fabulous fiber cookbook

fabulous fiber cookbook

Jeanne Jones

Preface by Kenneth W. Heaton, M.D.

Drawings by Cathy Greene

**101 Productions
San Francisco**

TO CHERI-BABY, MY SISTER
AND MY BEST FRIEND

In Grateful Acknowledgement:
Taita Pearn, M.S., R.D., for making the technical portions of this book possible
Carol Eastman for manuscript preparation
Lee Ann Jones for recipe preparation and testing
Deborah Mazzanti for sharing generously her knowledge and experience

Copyright © 1977 Jeanne Jones
Drawings copyright © 1977 Cathy Greene

Printed and bound in the United States of America.
Distributed to the book trade in the United States
by Charles Scribner's Sons, New York, and in Canada
by Van Nostrand Reinhold Ltd., Toronto

Published by 101 Productions
834 Mission Street
San Francisco, California 94103

Library of Congress Cataloging in Publication Data

Jones, Jeanne.
    Fabulous fiber cookbook.

    Bibliography: p.
    Includes index.
    1. High-fiber diet—Recipes.   2. Low-calorie diet—
Recipes.   I. Title.
RM237.6.J66   641.5'53   77-742
ISBN 0-89286-110-X
ISBN 0-89286-109-6 pbk.

contents

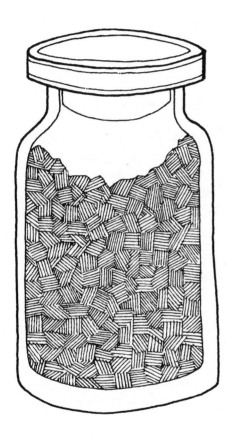

preface

In medical circles, dietary fibre is one of the most fashionable and fastest growing areas of research. What is all the excitement about?

The term fibre is a convenient shorthand for a family of complicated chemical substances known as polymers. It is for the specialist to worry about the names and properties of the individual members of the fibre family (cellulose, hemicelluloses or non-cellulosic polysaccharides, pectins, gums, lignins, waxes and cutins). For the ordinary food-lover and health-lover, the essential facts about fibre can be summed up in a few simple sentences: (1) Fibre is the tough material from which are made the cell walls of all plants. (2) All plant foods are rich in fibre, unless the food has been refined. Refining is any process which separates a fibre-rich fraction (which is generally thrown away or given to animals) from a starch-rich or sugar-rich fraction, which is sold as human food. The main examples of refined fibre-depleted foods in our modern diet are, firstly, white and brown sugars, syrups and molasses, which are all refined from sugar cane or sugar beet and, secondly, white flour plus all brown flours which are less than wholemeal, in other words all flours which contain less than the whole wheat grain. White rice, cornflour and most breakfast cereals also fall into the category of refined foods. (3) Fibre, being tough, forces the eater to chew his food. (4) Fibre cannot be digested by human digestive juices. This means it travels unscathed through the small intestine, and sweeps into the large intestine or colon—the only component of diet to do this in any quantity. In the large intestine, fibre has a gentle laxative effect, which can be summed up in the term "bowel relaxation."

All this may seem simple, even obvious. But its significance has only just begun to be appreciated by the medical profession. Great truths tend to be simple, but doctors are trained in so many complicated theories that they sometimes find it difficult to accept a simple idea.

Dr. T. L. Cleave's theory that refined carbohydrate foods cause many of the ills of civilisation is supremely logical, once the properties of fibre have been grasped. Since 1969, I have had the privilege of knowing this man, who was the first to realise that an extraordinarily wide range of diseases can be blamed on refined foods. Seeing all these diseases spring from a common cause, he had the daring idea of including them all as manifestations of a single master-disease. He called this master-disease the saccharine disease (pronounced to rhyme with the river Rhine), because saccharine literally means sugar-related and all carbohydrates are digested into sugars before being absorbed into the blood-stream. Perhaps there is a better name than saccharine disease, but I have yet to hear it.

Cleave's revolutionary conception begins with the inescapable fact that fibre is natural. Our bodies are adjusted to this "useless" part of our diet just as they are adjusted to the presence of "useless" nitrogen in the air. Air without nitrogen, that is pure oxygen, is dangerous to our bodies. So, says Cleave, is "purified" or fibre-depleted food. And in support of this idea he has amassed a wealth of historical and geographical evidence. This shows that there are many diseases which are common only if and when the diet contains refined carbohydrates. Most of these diseases fall into two groups—those due to overconsumption or excessive calorie intake, and diseases due to disordered function of the intestines.

The first group of diseases contains some of modern man's worst enemies—obesity, diabetes mellitus, gallstones and, above all, coronary artery disease. Cleave blames these, and I agree with him, more on refined sugar than on refined flour and other cereals. The reason is that sugar is particularly easy to consume. Being soluble in water it can be taken in drinks and swallowed without any effort at all, whereas refined cereal foods still have to be chewed to some extent. Moreover the sweetness of sugar is compulsively attractive to many people—a fact well-known to all food manufacturers (just look at the labels). Refined sugar and anything containing it is the arch-enemy of anyone who would keep his calorie intake down and so avoid the diseases of over-nutrition. Nature seems to know this, since it has ensured that in its natural state sweetness is always difficult to obtain. In all sweet-tasting fruits and roots, sugar (or rather a variety of sugars) is diluted with a good deal of water and above all, it is encased in a tough, fibrous cage. It is as if nature is telling us "chew sugar, or eschew it." In our society, the average man, woman and child consumes five ounces of sugar a day. This is possible only because the sugar is taken almost entirely in refined form. Were someone to take five ounces of sugar in natural, unrefined form, he would have to chew his way through nearly three pounds of apples or nearly two pounds of peeled bananas. If he succeeded in this feat, his intake of other foods would drop drastically. So we see that fibre looks after the calorie problem for us, simply by making calories harder to get.

The second group of diseases, those due to disordered function of the intestines, contains some more all-too-familiar ailments of civilised man. They may be less dramatic but they cause endless misery. They include simple constipation (with all the bloating, discomfort and indigestion which so often accompany it), haemorrhoids, diverticular disease and, in all probability, appendicitis. Less certainly, it can be argued that cancer of the large bowel is due in part to the small concentrated faeces of a low fibre, refined diet. There may be controversy over this, but there is no controversy at all about the remarkable beneficial effects of a high fibre diet on the badly behaved colon. The easiest, most efficient way to increase the fibre in the diet is to eat wholemeal bread, and if this is not enough, to add wheat bran to the diet. In Britain, these actions are now recommended by nine out of ten gastroenterologists to their patients with colon problems—a remarkable change from the early nineteen-seventies, when fibre had hardly been heard of.

I must emphasise that a genuine high fibre diet is not taking bran with everything. It is a diet which excludes all the fibre-depleted foods, including sugars or, rather, which replaces these refined products with natural unprocessed foods.

As a jaw-exercising calorie-stopper, and as an intestinal peace-maker, the potential of fibre is indeed fabulous. It needed a very special person to write a fibre cookbook worthy of its subject. And who else to do it but Jeanne Jones! In her previous books she has proved that healthy eating can be tasty eating. In this book she proves that it is exciting as well.

Kenneth W. Heaton, M.D., F.R.C.P.
Consultant Senior Lecturer in Medicine
University of Bristol
Bristol Royal Infirmary
Bristol, England

introduction

There is a very amusing aspect about all of the recent attention and widespread publicity being given to the fabulous "new" high fiber diet. Before 1870 and the invention of the roller mill the same high fiber unrefined diet was the "old" diet consumed by practically everyone. Only royalty and the extremely wealthy were able to afford the small amounts of white flour produced because the process used for refining was so time-consuming and costly. The majority of the people ate coarse, dark breads which came to be known as "peasants' bread." To this day, this type of bread is still referred to as "peasants' bread" in many parts of the world.

The roller mill made the separation of the bran, germ and the white inner substance of grain far more rapid and inexpensive so that an increasingly greater percentage of the population could afford to emulate the upper classes by switching over to refined white breads.

It took at least 50 years to discover that most of the important vitamins, minerals and fibers in grain were concentrated in the bran and germ which were either discarded or fed to animals.

In England during the periods of the two world wars in this century, unrefined flour was used in order to stretch the supply of grain. A general improvement in health was also noted during these periods. But for some unknown reason it failed to arouse much interest or bring about any noticeable change in diet education.

You will find another even more exciting concept of this "new" high fiber diet in your own realization of how quickly it will become the way you are eating by choice. You will find you actually prefer unrefined, natural foods not only because you will feel better and find it easier to control your weight eating them, but also that they are tastier and more interesting than their more refined counterparts.

Realizing the many advantages of this diet approach I couldn't wait to get started on this book to share with you what has become my own diet lifestyle. I hope you will have as much fun cooking and entertaining on a Fabulous Fiber Diet as I have had creating these recipes for you.

9

the fabulous fiber diet program

We are all hearing a great deal about the importance of fiber in our diets. Therefore, I think it is important to know what fiber is, where it comes from, why it is so important to our health and how we can adapt our own diets to contain an adequate amount of dietary fiber.

Dietary fiber is that fabulous indigestable part of plant food which is totally lacking in nutritional value, not absorbed by the body and does not supply calories for energy; therefore, it cannot make us fat. It does, however, add bulk to the diet because of its water-holding characteristics.

Our grandmothers often referred to dietary fiber as "roughage," but today many doctors prefer to call it "softage." When bran and other dietary fibers absorb water they swell, becoming soft and adding the necessary bulk needed to aid bowel function and help control constipation.

Unprocessed wheat bran, or miller's bran as it is often called, is currently the most talked about fiber food. It is of value in adding fiber to the diet and controlling constipation and diverticular disease. However, it is by no means the total answer to the possible benefits to be derived from a completely unrefined diet. It is more important to try to eliminate all refined carbohydrates from your diet and replace them with unrefined foods.

Good sources of fiber are found in whole grain flour, cereals and breads made from whole grain ingredients. Seeds and nuts contain fiber and so do fruits and vegetables.

When possible, eat fruits and vegetables raw and unpeeled. When you are going to cook them, serve them while they are still slightly crunchy or what I call "crisp tender."

Not only is a high fiber diet recommended for good general health and proper bowel function, recent research indicates that it may prevent many other diseases not before associated with a lack of fiber in the diet. These diseases include ulcerative colitis, cancer of the colon, diverticular diseases, appendicitis, hiatus hernia, diabetes, heart disease and high cholesterol, to name a few.

An unrefined, high fiber diet also offers a natural protection from obesity. According to Dr. Kenneth W. Heaton, consultant, senior lecturer in medicine at the University of Bristol Department of Medicine, Bristol Royal Infirmary in England, there are three different ways fiber acts as an obstacle to energy intake and obesity.

The first obstacle is that fiber must be chewed and that slows down digestion. The second is that fiber is space-filling and the third is that it promotes satiety or the satisfied feeling of having had enough to eat. In other words, you don't have "just enough room left" for one more piece of gooey pastry—you're full!

When you are eating an unrefined, high fiber diet the food you eat will pass through you and leave your system much more quickly than it does on a diet of refined, low fiber foods. This shorter transit time means that your body absorbs fewer calories from the foods you eat and serves as still another aid in controlling your weight.

11

the fabulous fiber diet program

How much fiber should be added to the daily diet? This is still an extremely controversial question. There is such a broad range of opinion among the medical experts in the field that I think the "middle of the road" approach is probably the best.

When adding unprocessed wheat bran to the diet, between 7 and 15 grams of bran per day are the most frequently recommended amounts. Most doctors recommend raising the bran intake slowly, starting with a small amount and increasing it until desired results are achieved.

Try to totally eliminate white flour and other refined grains from your diet. Avoid buying "instant" anything. You can count on its being more refined than its old-fashioned, slow-cooking counterpart. Read all labels carefully and try not to purchase products containing refined grains, sugar or preservatives.

In trying to eliminate refined carbohydrates as much as possible from all of the recipes in this book I have regularly replaced sugar, molasses, syrup and honey with date "sugar." Date "sugar" is not really a sugar at all, although it looks like and tastes very much like brown sugar. It is made from dried dates finely ground to the consistency of coarse sugar. It has the advantage of being allowed in sugar-restricted diets since it is really just a ground up fruit. In the diabetic diet one tablespoon of date "sugar" equals one Fruit Exchange.

Many people have asked me why I prefer date "sugar" to honey which is also a natural food. My answer is simple: Honey, although a natural carbohydrate, is a refined carbohydrate. It is refined by bees for bees and it contains no fiber. Date "sugar" is not a refined carbohydrate and it does contain fiber. One tablespoon of honey contains 60 calories and 0 fiber. One tablespoon of date "sugar" contains 40 calories and .5 gram of fiber. From this comparison it is easy to see why date "sugar" is a better sweetener for a high fiber, low calorie diet than honey.

Date "sugar" is available in some markets and practically all health and natural food stores. If you are unable to find it elsewhere write to Box 1212, La Jolla, California 92038 for information.

All of the recipes in this book are designed to make increasing the fiber content of your diet an exciting, new approach to gourmet cooking and elegant entertaining.

At the end of this chapter you will find a 7-Day Fabulous Fiber Diet. It is designed to help you with your own personal diet program and also as a guide for party planning.

FRUITS

Each portion below contains
approximately:
10 grams of carbohydrate
40 calories

$\frac{gm}{fiber}$ = grams of fiber

*	good source of vitamin C
**	good source of vitamin A
***	good source of vitamins A and C

gm
fiber

gm fiber	
1.0	Apple: 1 2 inches in diameter
.1	Apple juice: 1/2 cup
.6	Applesauce, unsweetened: 1/2 cup
.6	Apricots, fresh: 2 medium**
.5	Apricots, dried: 3 halves**
	Avocado: see Fats list
.3	Banana: 1/2 small
3.0	Blackberries: 3/4 cup
1.5	Blueberries: 2/3 cup
.3	Cantaloupe: 1/4 6 inches in diameter***
.3	Cherries, sweet: 10 large
.3	Crenshaw melon: 2-inch wedge
.5	Dates: 2
.5	Date "sugar": 1 tablespoon
.6	Figs, fresh: 1 large
.8	Figs, dried: 1 large
.2	Grapefruit: 1/2 4 inches in diameter*
trace	Grapefruit juice: 1/2 cup*
.4	Grapes: 12 large

.2	Grapes, Thompson seedless: 20 grapes
trace	Grape juice: 1/4 cup
4.4	Guava: 2/3*
.7	Honeydew melon: 1/4 5 inches in diameter
3.0	Kumquats: 2
trace	Lemon juice: 1/2 cup
trace	Lime juice: 1/2 cup
.5	Loquats: 3
.2	Lychees, fresh: 3
.9	Mango: 1/2 small**
.3	Nectarine: 1 medium
.5	Orange: 1 small*
.1	Orange juice: 1/2 cup*
1.0	Papaya: 1/3 medium*
1.5	Passion fruit: 1
.1	Passion fruit juice: 1/3 cup
.6	Peach: 1 medium
1.0	Pear: 1 small
.8	Persimmon: 1/2 medium
.3	Pineapple, fresh or canned without sugar: 1/2 cup
trace	Pineapple juice: 1/3 cup
.2	Plantain: 1/2 small
.3	Plums: 2 medium
.2	Pomegranate: 1 small
.3	Prunes, fresh or dried: 2
trace	Prune juice: 1/4 cup
.2	Raisins: 2 tablespoons
3.0	Raspberries: 1/2 cup
1.5	Strawberries: 3/4 cup
.5	Tangerines: 1 large or 2 small
.2	Tomato catsup: 3 tablespoons
.5	Watermelon: 3/4 cup

the fabulous fiber diet program

VEGETABLES

Each portion below equals 1 cup unless otherwise specified and contains approximately:

5 grams of carbohydrate
2 grams of protein
25 calories

$\frac{gm}{fiber}$ = grams of fiber

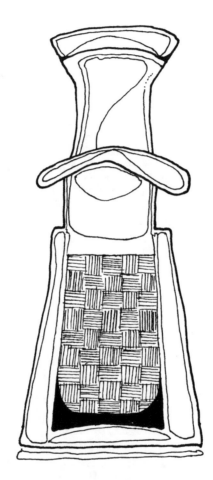

$\frac{gm}{fiber}$	
.6	Alfalfa sprouts
4.8	Artichoke, whole, base and ends of leaves (1)
1.0	Asparagus
.7	Bean sprouts
.8	Beets (1/2 cup)
1.3	Beet greens†
1.5	Broccoli***
1.6	Brussels sprouts*
.8	Cabbage*
1.0	Carrots (medium, 1)**
1.0	Cauliflower†
.6	Celery†
.7	Celery root (1/2 cup)
.9	Chard†
.8	Chayote
.9	Chicory**†
2.0	Chilies
1.4	Cilantro†
1.2	Chives***
.9	Collard*†
1.6	Cranberries
.6	Cucumbers
1.6	Dandelion greens†
1.8	Eggplant

1.2	Endive†
1.0	Escarole**†
.5	Green beans, mature (1/2 cup)
1.0	Green onion tops
.5	Jerusalem artichokes (1/2 cup)
1.2	Kale*†
.7	Leeks (1/2 cup)
.6	Lettuce†
1.8	Lima beans, baby (1/4 cup)
.8	Mushrooms†
.9	Mustard, fresh*†
1.0	Okra
.6	Onions (1/2 cup)
1.2	Palm heart
1.5	Parsley***†
1.5	Peas (1/2 cup)
1.5	Peppers, green and red*
.9	Poke†
1.3	Pumpkin (1/2 cup)*
.7	Radishes†
.9	Rhubarb†
.7	Romaine lettuce†
1.1	Rutabagas (1/2 cup)
.9	Spinach†
1.2	Squash, acorn (1/2 cup)
1.4	Squash, Hubbard (1/2 cup)
1.2	String beans
1.2	Summer squash
.9	Tomatoes
.1	Tomato catsup (1-1/2 tablespoons)
.4	Tomato juice (1/2 cup)
.5	Tomato paste (3 tablespoons)
.6	Tomato sauce (1/2 cup)
.8	Turnips (1/2 cup)
.3	V-8 juice (2/3 cup)**
.2	Water chestnuts (medium, 4)
.7	Watercress**†
1.4	Zucchini squash

*	good source of vitamin C
**	good source of vitamin A
***	good source of vitamins A and C
†	calories negligible when eaten raw

14

STARCHES

Each portion below contains approximately:

15 grams of carbohydrate
2 grams of protein
70 calories

$\frac{gm}{fiber}$ = grams of fiber

$\frac{gm}{fiber}$	VEGETABLES
1.4	Beans, dried, cooked (lima, soya, navy, kidney): 1/2 cup
.5	Beans, baked, without pork: 1/4 cup
.6	Corn, on-the-cob: 1 4 inches long
.6	Corn, cooked and drained: 1/3 cup
.1	Hominy: 1/2 cup
.7	Lentils, dried, cooked: 1/2 cup
2.0	Parsnips: 1 small
.5	Peas, dry, cooked, black-eyed, split: 1/2 cup
.3	Poi: 1/2 cup
.7	Potatoes, sweet, yams: 1/4 cup**
.5	Potatoes, white, baked or boiled: 1 2 inches in diameter
.5	Potatoes, white, mashed: 1/2 cup
.2	Potato chips: 15 2 inches in diameter
2.6	Pumpkin, canned: 1 cup
.2	Rice, brown, cooked: 1/3 cup
trace	Rice, white, cooked: 1/2 cup
.2	Tomato catsup, commercial: 3 tablespoons

** good source of vitamin A

$\frac{gm}{fiber}$	BREADS
trace	Bagel: 1/2
trace	Biscuit: 1 2 inches in diameter
.1	Bread, rye: 1 slice
.4	Bread, whole wheat: 1 slice
trace	Bread (white and sourdough): 1 slice
trace	Breadsticks: 4 9 inches long
trace	Bun, hamburger: 1/2
trace	Bun, hot dog: 2/3
.1	Corn bread: 1 piece 1-1/2 inches square
.3	Cracked wheat (bulgur): 1-1/2 tablespoons
trace	Croutons, plain: 1/2 cup
trace	English muffin: 1/2
trace	Melba toast: 6 slices
trace	Muffin, unsweetened: 1 2 inches in diameter
trace	Matzo cracker, plain: 1 6 inches in diameter
trace	Pancakes: 2 3 inches in diameter
trace	Popover: 1
trace	Roll: 1 2 inches in diameter
trace	Rusks: 2
.1	Spoon bread: 1/2 cup
.3	Tortilla, corn: 1 6 inches in diameter
trace	Tortilla, flour: 1 8 inches in diameter
trace	Waffle: 1 4 inches in diameter

$\frac{gm}{fiber}$	CEREALS
2.4	All-Bran: 1/2 cup
2.0	Bran Flakes: 1/2 cup
3.3	Bran, unprocessed rice: 1/3 cup
3.2	Bran, unprocessed wheat: 1/3 cup
.2	Cheerios: 1 cup
.2	Concentrate: 1/4 cup
.1	Corn flakes: 2/3 cup
.1	Cornmeal, cooked: 1/2 cup
trace	Cream-of-Wheat, cooked: 1/2 cup
.4	Grapenuts: 1/4 cup
.3	Grapenut Flakes: 1/2 cup
.1	Grits, cooked: 1/2 cup
trace	Kix: 3/4 cup
.3	Life: 1/2 cup
trace	Malt-O-Meal, cooked: 1/2 cup
trace	Maypo, cooked: 1/2 cup
trace	Matzo meal, cooked: 1/2 cup
.2	Oatmeal, cooked: 1/2 cup
.2	Pep, 1/2 cup
.2	Puffed rice: 1-1/2 cups
.3	Puffed wheat: 1-1/2 cups
trace	Rice Krispies: 2/3 cup
.4	Shredded wheat, biscuit: 1 large
.3	Special K: 1-1/4 cups
.2	Steel cut oats, cooked: 1/2 cup
.4	Wheat Chex: 1/2 cup
trace	Wheat germ, defatted: 1 ounce or 3 tablespoons
.2	Wheaties: 2/3 cup

the fabulous fiber diet program

gm fiber CRACKERS

trace	Animal: 8
trace	Arrowroot: 3
trace	Cheese tidbits: 3/4 cup
.2	Graham: 2
trace	Oyster: 20 or 1/2 cup
trace	Pretzels: 10 very thin, or 1 large
trace	Saltines: 5
trace	Soda: 3
trace	Ritz: 6
.3	RyKrisp: 3
.3	Rye thins: 10
trace	Triangle thins: 14
trace	Vegetable thins: 12
trace	Wheat thins: 12

gm fiber FLOURS

trace	Arrowroot: 2 tablespoons
trace	All-purpose: 2-1/2 tablespoons
trace	Bisquick: 1-1/2 tablespoons
3.2	Bran, unprocessed wheat: 5 tablespoons
.3	Buckwheat: 3 tablespoons
trace	Cake: 2-1/2 tablespoons
.1	Cornmeal: 3 tablespoons
trace	Cornstarch: 2 tablespoons
trace	Matzo meal: 3 tablespoons
trace	Potato flour: 2-1/2 tablespoons
.5	Rye, dark: 4 tablespoons
.6	Whole wheat: 3 tablespoons
trace	Noodles, macaroni, spaghetti, cooked: 1/2 cup
trace	Noodles, dry, egg: 3-1/2 ounces
trace	Noodles, cooked, egg: 3-1/2 ounces

gm fiber MISCELLANEOUS

1.8	Cocoa, dry, unsweetened: 2-1/2 tablespoons
.3	Date "Sugar" Ice Milk: 1/4 cup
0	Ice cream, low-saturated: 1/2 cup
.3	Popcorn, popped, unbuttered: 1-1/2 cups
.2	Potato chips, Fritos: 3/4 ounce or 1/2 cup

PROTEINS

Each portion below
contains approximately:
7 grams of protein
5 grams of fat
75 calories

gm fiber = grams of fiber

✓ low in fats
(subtract 2 grams of fat and
20 calories)

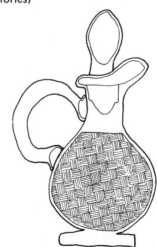

gm fiber CHEESE

0	American: 1 ounce
0	Blue: 1 ounce or 1/4 cup, crumbled
0	Cheddar: 1 ounce
0	Cottage cheese, creamed: 1/4 cup
0	Cottage cheese, low fat: 1/3 cup ✓
0	Edam: 1 ounce
0	Farmer: 1/4 cup, crumbled ✓
0	Feta: 1 ounce
0	Hoop: 1/4 cup ✓
0	Liederkranz: 1 ounce
0	Monterey Jack: 1 ounce
0	Mozzarella: 1 ounce
0	Muenster: 1 ounce
0	Parmesan: 1/4 cup, 2/3 ounce or 4 tablespoons
trace	Pimiento cheese spread: 1 ounce
0	Pot cheese: 1/4 cup ✓
0	Ricotta, regular: 1/4 cup or 2 ounces
0	Ricotta, part skim: 1/4 cup or 2 ounces ✓
0	Romano: 1/4 cup, 2/3 ounce or 4 tablespoons
0	Roquefort: 1 ounce or 1/4 cup, crumbled
0	Stilton: 1 ounce or 1/4 cup, crumbled
0	Swiss: 1 ounce

gm fiber EGGS

0	Eggs, medium: 1

gm fiber   PEANUT BUTTER

.3   Peanut butter: 2 tablespoons

gm fiber   FISH AND SEAFOOD

0   Abalone: 1-1/3 ounces ✓
0   Albacore, canned in oil: 1 ounce ✓
0   Anchovy fillets: 9 ✓
0   Bass: 1-1/2 ounces ✓
0   Caviar: 1 ounce ✓
0   Clams, fresh: 3 large or 1-1/2 ounces ✓
0   Clams, canned: 1-1/2 ounces ✓
0   Clam juice: 1-1/2 cups ✓
0   Cod: 1 ounce ✓
0   Crab, canned: 1/2 ounce ✓
0   Crab, cracked, fresh: 1-1/2 ounces ✓
0   Flounder: 1-2/3 ounces ✓
0   Frog legs: 2 large or 3 ounces ✓
0   Halibut: 1 ounce or 1 piece 2 x 2 x 1 inches ✓
0   Herring, pickled: 1-1/4 ounces ✓
0   Lobster, fresh: 1-1/2 ounces, 1/4 cup or 1/4 small lobster ✓
0   Lobster, canned: 1-1/2 ounces ✓
0   Oysters, fresh: 3 medium or 1-1/2 ounces ✓
0   Oysters, canned: 1-1/2 ounces ✓
0   Perch: 1-1/2 ounces ✓
0   Red snapper: 1-1/2 ounces ✓
0   Salmon: 1 ounce ✓
0   Salmon, canned: 1-1/2 ounces ✓
0   Sand dabs: 1-1/2 ounces ✓
0   Sardines: 4 small ✓
0   Scallops: 3 medium or 1-1/2 ounces ✓

0   Sole: 1-2/3 ounces ✓
0   Shrimp, fresh: 5 medium ✓
0   Shrimp, canned: 5 medium or 1-1/2 ounces ✓
0   Swordfish: 1-1/2 ounces ✓
0   Trout: 1-1/2 ounces ✓
0   Tuna: 1 ounce ✓
0   Tuna, canned: 1/4 cup ✓
0   Turbot: 1-1/2 ounces ✓

gm fiber   PORK

0   Bacon (see Fats): 1 slice
0   Canadian bacon: 1 slice 2-1/2 inches in diameter, 1/4 inch thick
0   Chops: 1/2 small chop or 1 ounce
0   Ham, lean: 1 ounce or 1 slice 3 x 2 x 1/8 inches ✓
0   Liver: 1 ounce
0   Roast, lean: 1 ounce, 1 slice 3 x 2 x 1/8 inches or 1/4 cup, chopped
0   Sausage: 2 small or 1 ounce
0   Spareribs, without fat: meat from 3 medium or 1 ounce

gm fiber   VEAL

0   Chop: 1/2 small or 1 ounce ✓
0   Cutlet: 1 ounce or 1 slice 3 x 2 x 1/8 inches ✓
0   Calves' liver: 1 ounce or 1 slice 3 x 2 x 1/8 inches
0   Roast: 1 ounce or 1 slice 3 x 2 x 1/8 inches ✓
0   Sweetbreads: 1 ounce, 1/4 pair or 1/4 cup, chopped

gm fiber   BEEF

0   Brains: 1 ounce
0   Brisket: 1 ounce
0   Corned beef, canned: 1 ounce or 1 slice 3 x 2 x 1/8 inches
0   Flank steak: 1-1/3 ounces ✓
0   Frankfurters: 1/2 pound (8 to 9 per pound)
0   Hamburger, very lean (4 ounces raw = 3 ounces cooked): 1 ounce
0   Heart: 1 ounce or 1 slice 3 x 2 x 1/8 inches
0   Kidney: 1 ounce or 1 slice 2 x 3 x 1/8 inches
0   Liver: 1 ounce or 1 slice 2 x 3 x 1/8 inches
0   Rib roast: 1 ounce, 1/4 cup, chopped, or 1 slice 2 x 3 x 1/8 inches ✓
0   Short ribs, very lean: 1 rib or 1 ounce
0   Steak, very lean (filet mignon, New York, sirloin, T-bone): 1 ounce or 1 slice 3 x 2 x 1/8 inches ✓
0   Tongue: 1 slice 3 x 2 x 1/4 inches
0   Tripe: 1 ounce or 1 piece 5 x 2 inches ✓

gm fiber   LAMB

0   Chops, lean: 1/2 small chop or 1 ounce ✓
0   Roast, lean: 1 ounce, 1 slice 3 x 2 x 1/8 inches or 1/4 cup, chopped ✓

the fabulous fiber diet program

CHICKEN

0   Broiled or roasted: 1 ounce
    or 1 slice 3 x 2 x 1/8 inches ✓

0   Breast, without skin: 1/2
    small, 1 ounce or 1/4
    cup, chopped ✓

0   Heart: 1 ounce

0   Leg: 1/2 medium or 1 ounce ✓

0   Liver: 1 medium or 1 ounce

DUCK

0   Roasted, without skin: 1 ounce
    or 1 slice 3 x 2 x 1/8 inches

0   Wild duck, without skin:
    1/4 small

TURKEY

0   Meat, without skin: 1 ounce
    or 1 slice 3 x 2 x 1/8 inches ✓

OTHER POULTRY AND
GAME

0   Buffalo: 1 ounce or 1 slice
    3 x 2 x 1/8 inches ✓

0   Cornish game hen, without
    skin: 1/4 bird or 1 ounce ✓

0   Pheasant: 1-1/2 ounces ✓

0   Rabbit: 1 ounce or 1 slice
    3 x 2 x 1/8 inches ✓

0   Quail, without skin: 1/4 bird
    or 1 ounce ✓

0   Squab, without skin: 1/4 bird
    or 1 ounce ✓

0   Venison, lean, roast or steak:
    1 ounce or 1 slice 3 x 2 x
    1/8 inches ✓

COLD CUTS

0   Bologna: 1 ounce or 1 slice
    4-1/2 inches in diameter,
    1/8 inch thick

0   Liverwurst: 1 slice 3 inches in
    diameter, 1/4 inch thick

0   Spam: 1 ounce

0   Salami: 1 ounce or 1 slice
    4 inches in diameter, 1/3 inch
    thick

0   Vienna sausage: 2-1/2 sausages
    or 1 ounce

MILK

gm
fiber = grams of fiber

Each portion below contains
approximately:
12 grams of carbohydrate
8 grams of protein
trace of fat
80 calories

0   Milk, powdered, skim: 1/4 cup

0   Milk, skim, non-fat: 1 cup

0   Milk, evaporated, skim: 1/2 cup

0   Buttermilk: 1 cup

0   Yogurt, plain, non-fat: 1 cup

Each portion below contains
approximately:
12 grams of carbohydrate
8 grams of protein
5 grams of fat
125 calories

0   Milk, low-fat, 2% fat: 1 cup

0   Yogurt, plain, low-fat: 1 cup

Each portion below contains
approximately:
12 grams of carbohydrate
8 grams of protein
10 grams of fat
180 calories

0   Milk, whole: 1 cup

0   Milk, evaporated, whole: 1/2 cup

0   Ice Milk: 1 cup

FATS

Each portion below contains
approximately:
5 grams of fat
45 calories

gm
fiber = grams of fiber

.8 Avocado: 1/8 4 inches in
    diameter

0   Bacon, crisp: 1 slice

0   Butter: 1 teaspoon

1.2 Caraway seeds: 2 tablespoons

1.2 Cardamom seeds: 2 tablespoons

0   Chocolate, bitter: 1/3 ounce
    or 1/3 square

0   Cream cheese: 1 tablespoon

0	Cream, light, coffee: 2 tablespoons
0	Cream, heavy, whipping: 1 tablespoon
0	Cream, half-and-half: 3 tablespoons
0	Cream, sour: 2 tablespoons
0	Cream, sour, imitation: 2 tablespoons (Imo, Matey)
0	Margarine, polyunsaturated: 1 teaspoon
0	Mayonnaise: 1 teaspoon
0	Oils, polyunsaturated: 1 teaspoon
.6	Olives: 5 small
.8	Poppy seeds, 1-1/2 tablespoons
.2	Pumpkin seeds, 1-1/2 teaspoons
	Salad dressings, commercial
trace	French oil and vinegar: 1-1/2 teaspoons
trace	Roquefort: 1 teaspoon
trace	Thousand Island (egg-free): 1 teaspoon
	Sauces, commercial
trace	Béarnaise: 1 teaspoon
trace	Hollandaise: 1 teaspoon
trace	Tartar sauce: 1 teaspoon
.2	Sesame seeds: 2 teaspoons
.2	Sunflower seeds: 1-1/4 teaspoons

NUTS (gm fiber)

.3	Almonds: 7
.2	Brazil nuts: 2
.2	Cashews: 7
.5	Coconut, fresh: 1 piece 1 x 1 x 3/8 inches
.3	Coconut, shredded, unsweetened: 2 tablespoons
1.2	Filberts: 5
1.2	Hazelnuts: 5
.1	Hickory nuts: 7 small
.3	Macadamia nuts: 2
.4	Peanuts: 10
.3	Pecans: 6 halves
.2	Pine nuts: 1 tablespoon
.1	Pistachio nuts: 15
.2	Soy nuts, toasted: 3 tablespoons
.2	Walnuts, black: 5 halves
.2	Walnuts, California: 5 halves

HERBS, SPICES, SEASONINGS, ETC.

Calories are negligible and need not be counted in the following list. An excess of many of these foods, however, is not good for you.

gm/fiber = grams of fiber

0	Coffee
0	Tea
0	Clear broth
0	Consommé and bouillon (fat-free)
trace	Lemon
0	Gelatin (unsweetened)
0	Rennet tablets
trace	Pickles (without sugar)
trace	Mustard

0	Extracts
0	Angostura bitters
0	Salt
0	Soy sauce
0	Vinegar

Herbs and Spices

.4	Allspice, 1 teaspoon
.2	Basil, 1 teaspoon
.3	Bay leaf, ground, 1 teaspoon
.2	Celery seed, 1 teaspoon
.5	Chili powder, 1/2 teaspoon
.3	Cinnamon, 1 teaspoon
.4	Coriander, 1 teaspoon
.1	Cumin seed, 1 teaspoon
.4	Dill seed, 1 teaspoon
.4	Fennel seed, 1 teaspoon
trace	Garlic powder, 1 teaspoon
trace	Ginger, powdered, 1 teaspoon
trace	Mace, 1 teaspoon
.2	Marjoram, 1 teaspoon
trace	Mint
trace	Nutmeg, 1 teaspoon
.1	Onion powder, 1 teaspoon
.4	Paprika, 1 teaspoon
.1	Parsley flakes, 1 teaspoon
.2	Pepper, black, 1 teaspoon
.5	Pepper, red, 1 teaspoon
.1	Pepper, white, 1 teaspoon
.2	Rosemary, 1 teaspoon
.1	Sage, 1 teaspoon
.2	Savory, 1 teaspoon
.1	Tarragon, 1 teaspoon
.1	Thyme, 1 teaspoon
.1	Turmeric, 1 teaspoon

7-day fabulous fiber diet

The 7-Day Fabulous Fiber Diet offers menu suggestions for approximately 1000 calories per day and at least 7 grams of fiber. Of course, all of the menus can be used for all calorie and fiber levels by slight additions or deletions.

To calculate your own fiber totals in recipes, add up the grams of fiber in all of the ingredients and divide by the number of servings you are making.

DAY & TOTALS	BREAKFAST	LUNCH	DINNER

1
 	
8.0 grams of fiber
 	
1014 calories
	1/2 grapefruit
	1 egg, boiled
	1 slice Bran-Raisin Bread
	1 T. unprocessed wheat bran
	  mixed with
	1/2 cup non-fat milk
	coffee or tea
	1.4 grams of fiber
	241 calories
		1 serving Jeanne Appleseed Salad
		1/2 Roughage Roll, toasted
		1 T. unprocessed wheat bran
		  mixed with
		1/4 cup non-fat milk
		coffee or tea
		2.8 grams of fiber
		427 calories
			1 serving Tropical Ham Slices
			1/2 cup Curried Cauliflower
			1/2 cup steamed spinach
			2/3 cup blueberries with
			1/4 cup non-fat milk
			coffee or tea
			3.8 grams of fiber
			346 calories

2
 	
7.4 grams of fiber
 	
942 calories
	1/2 cup Powerful Porridge with
	1/4 low-fat cottage cheese
	1/2 cup non-fat plain yogurt
	coffee or tea
	1.4 grams of fiber
	269 calories
		1 serving Salmon-Anchovy Aspic
		1 cup shredded lettuce
		1/4 cup Dilled Onions Lautrec
		1/2 slice Whole Wheat Bread
		1/4 cantaloupe
		1/2 cup non-fat milk
		coffee or tea
		2.4 grams of fiber
		334 calories
			1 serving Cold Curried
			  Grapefruit Soup
			1 serving Vegetable Medley
			  au Gratin
			1/2 slice Sunflower Seed Bread
			1/2 cup non-fat milk
			coffee or tea
			3.6 grams of fiber
			339 calories

3 8.2 grams of fiber 1045 calories	1/2 banana, sliced, on 1/3 cup whole bran cereal with 1/2 cup non-fat milk 2 ounces lean ham coffee or tea **2.7 grams of fiber** **260 calories**	1 serving Quiche Mary Ann 1 cup steamed asparagus on 1 cup shredded lettuce 3/4 cup strawberries with 1/2 cup non-fat milk coffee or tea **3.7 grams of fiber** **424 calories**	1 serving Pizza Chicken 1 cup spinach with 1 T. Italian Fiber Dressing 1 small bunch grapes coffee or tea **1.8 grams of fiber** **361 calories**

	BREAKFAST	LUNCH	DINNER
DAY & TOTALS **4** 8.7 grams of fiber 984 calories	1/2 cup orange juice 1 serving Wheat Germ Waffles 1-1/2 t. Date Butter 1 T. unprocessed wheat bran mixed with 1/4 cup non-fat milk coffee or tea **2.5 grams of fiber** **394 calories**	1 serving Cheddar Cheese Soup 1/2 Roughage Roll 1 cup shredded lettuce and 1/2 apple, sliced, with 2 T. High-Low Dressing and 1 T. unprocessed wheat bran coffee or tea **2.4 grams of fiber** **348 calories**	3 servings Oyster Ceviche 3 Toasted Tortilla Triangles 1/2 cup raspberries with 1/2 cup non-fat milk coffee or tea **3.8 grams of fiber** **242 calories**
DAY & TOTALS **5** 8.2 grams of fiber 1017 calories	1/4 cantaloupe 1 egg, boiled 1 slice Whole Wheat Bread 2 T. unprocessed wheat bran mixed with 1/2 cup non-fat milk coffee or tea **2.0 grams of fiber** **256 calories**	1 Nut Burger 1 serving Hawaiian Cole Slaw on 1/2 cup shredded lettuce 2 T. unprocessed wheat bran and 1-1/2 t. Date "Sugar" mixed with 1/2 cup non-fat plain yogurt coffee or tea **3.3 grams of fiber** **439 calories**	1 serving Company Lamb Chops 1 cup steamed broccoli 1 cup shredded lettuce and 1/2 cup chopped tomato with 2 T. High-Low Dressing 1/2 cup non-fat milk coffee or tea **3.1 grams of fiber** **322 calories**

DAY & TOTALS
6
 	
9.7 grams of fiber
 	
994 calories
	1/2 cup raspberries with
	1/2 cup low-fat cottage cheese
	2 T. unprocessed wheat bran
	   mixed with
	1/2 cup non-fat milk
	coffee or tea
	4.2 grams of fiber
	206 calories
		1 serving Sportsman Salad
		1 slice Wheat Berry Bread,
		   toasted
		1 Frozen Bonbon
		coffee or tea
		2.7 grams of fiber
		389 calories
			1 serving Sherried Chicken and
			   Mushrooms on Rice
			1 serving Brussels Sprouts in
			   Herb Butter
			1 small pear
			1/4 cup non-fat milk
			coffee or tea
			2.8 grams of fiber
			399 calories

DAY & TOTALS
7
 	
8.2 grams of fiber
 	
1033 calories
	1 serving See's Soufflé-Squares
	1-1/2 t. Date Butter
	2/3 cup blueberries and
	2 T. unprocessed wheat bran
	   mixed with
	1/2 cup non-fat milk
	coffee or tea
	3.0 grams of fiber
	252 calories
		1 serving Hubert's Sunday
		   Sandwich
		1 T. unprocessed wheat bran and
		1-1/2 t. Date "Sugar" mixed with
		1/2 cup non-fat plain yogurt
		coffee or tea
		2.4 grams of fiber
		400 calories
			1 Tostada
			1 serving Bran-Mango Mousse
			coffee or tea
			2.8 grams of fiber
			381 calories

stocks, bouillons and consommes

Once you get in the habit of making your own stocks, you will find it takes little time and makes a great difference in the flavor of all your other recipes. Also, when you make your own stocks, bouillons and consommés, you are sure of the quality of the ingredients and that the result is completely fat free and without additives.

Making your own stock is much less expensive than powdered stock base, bouillon cubes or canned bouillon and consommés. To economize even more, keep a couple of big plastic bags in your freezer for bones and meat scraps, one for beef and veal and the other for poultry. Lamb, ham and pork bones may also be saved for making stock, but do not make good all-purpose stocks because their flavor is too pronounced.

Store your stock in the freezer. Freeze some of it in one-cup containers and some in ice cube trays (two ice cubes = one-fourth cup) for times when only a small amount is needed.

This is the only section in this book where you will find recipes which are not high in dietary fiber. The reason is that your basic stocks are not generally served alone but are used as ingredients in other recipes.

FISH STOCK

2 pounds fish heads, bones and trimmings
2-1/2 quarts water
2 onions, sliced
5 parsley sprigs
1 carrot, sliced
1/2 teaspoon marjoram

4 peppercorns
1 teaspoon salt
1 tablespoon fresh lemon juice

Makes 2 quarts (8 cups)
Calories negligible when defatted

Bring all of the ingredients to a boil and simmer for 40 minutes. Line a colander or strainer with damp cheesecloth and strain the fish stock through it. Cool and keep refrigerated. If you are not planning to use the fish stock within 2 days, freeze it.

stocks, bouillons and consommes

BEEF STOCK

3 pounds beef or veal bones
1 pound beef (optional)
2 carrots, cut in pieces
2 celery stalks, without leaves
1 onion, cut in half
1 tomato, cut in half
3 garlic buds
2 parsley sprigs
2 whole cloves

1/4 teaspoon thyme
1/4 teaspoon marjoram
1 bay leaf
10 peppercorns
1 teaspoon salt
defatted beef drippings (optional)

Makes about 2-1/2 quarts (10 cups)
Calories negligible when defatted

In a large pot or soup kettle, put the bones and enough cold water to cover by 1 inch. Bring to a boil, then lower heat and simmer slowly for 5 minutes; remove any scum that forms on the top. Add remaining ingredients and enough additional water to cover by 1 inch. Cover, leaving the lid ajar about 1 inch to allow the steam to escape and simmer very slowly for at least 5 hours. Ten hours are even better, if you will be around to turn off the heat! When the stock has finished cooking, allow it to come to room temperature and put it in the refrigerator, uncovered, overnight. When the fat has hardened on the surface it can be easily removed. After removing every bit of fat, warm the stock until it becomes liquid. Strain the liquid and add more salt to taste, if needed.

If the flavor of the stock is too weak, boil it down to evaporate more of the liquid and concentrate its strength. Store the stock in the freezer.

BROWN STOCK

The ingredients for Brown Stock are the same as for Beef Stock. Preheat oven to 400°. Brown bones and meat for 30 minutes. Add carrots, celery and onion and brown together for another 30 minutes, or until a rich brown in color. Put the browned meat and vegetables in a large pot with the remaining ingredients, adding cold water to cover by 1 inch. Cover, leaving the lid ajar about 1 inch to allow the steam to escape, and simmer very slowly for at least 5 hours. Proceed exactly as you do for Beef Stock.

CHICKEN STOCK

3 pounds chicken parts, wings, backs, etc.
1 whole stewing chicken (optional)
2 carrots, cut in pieces
2 celery stalks, without leaves
1 onion, cut in half
2 garlic buds
1 bay leaf

1/4 teaspoon basil
8 peppercorns
1 teaspoon salt

Makes about 2-1/2 quarts (10 cups)
Calories negligible when defatted

Put the chicken parts, whole chicken (if you are going to cook one), vegetables and spices in an 8- to 10-quart pot or soup kettle. Add cold water to cover by 1 inch. Bring slowly to a boil. Cover, leaving lid ajar about 1 inch to allow steam to escape. Simmer very slowly for 3 hours or until whole chicken is tender. Remove chicken and continue to simmer stock for 3 or 4 hours. Cool stock to room temperature and proceed exactly as you do for Beef Stock, preceding. Cooking the stewing chicken is helpful in two ways. First, it adds flavor to the stock. And second, it gives you a beautifully seasoned chicken for your dinner or for many other dishes, hot or cold.

TURKEY STOCK

1 turkey carcass
1 onion, cut in quarters
1 carrot, cut in pieces
2 bay leaves
1/2 teaspoon basil
1/4 teaspoon thyme
1/4 teaspoon marjoram

1 teaspoon salt
8 peppercorns
defatted turkey drippings (optional)

Makes 1-1/2 to 2 quarts (6 to 8 cups)
Calories negligible when defatted

Break up the turkey carcass and put it in an 8- to 10-quart pot or soup kettle. Add the vegetables and spices and cold water to cover by 1 inch. Cover, leaving the lid ajar about 1 inch to allow the steam to escape. Simmer slowly for 4 hours. Cool to room temperature and proceed exactly as you do for Beef Stock, preceding.

stocks, bouillons and consommes

COURT BOUILLON

4 cups water
1/4 cup white vinegar
1/2 lemon, sliced
1 celery stalk, without leaves, sliced
1 carrot, sliced
1/2 onion, sliced
1 garlic bud

1 bay leaf
6 peppercorns
1-1/2 teaspoons salt

Makes 1 quart (4 cups)
Calories negligible

Anytime you are going to poach shrimp, crab, lobster or any fish, prepare a court bouillon first. Of course you can use fish stock for poaching fish, but this court bouillon is much faster and easier to make and completely satisfactory. You just cannot compare seafood cooked in plain, salted water to the seafood cooked in court bouillon. Always be careful not to overcook seafood because overcooking makes it tough. For example, when cooking shrimp never allow them to boil more than 2 minutes. Then cool them in the court bouillon.

Combine all of the above ingredients and cook for 45 minutes. This court bouillon may be made ahead and reused many times. When doing this, strain before storing. After each use, store in the freezer.

CHICKEN OR BEEF BOUILLON

1 part Chicken Stock, page 25
   or Beef Stock, page 24

1 part water

Calories negligible

Put the stock and water in a pan and bring to a boil. Simmer for at least 15 minutes before using. Basically, bouillons are just weak stocks. For this reason I find it troublesome and confusing to actually make both stocks and bouillons from scratch. Troublesome, because the bouillon made from a good, rich stock has a better flavor than most other bouillons, and confusing because I have enough trouble keeping track of everything in my freezer as it is. Bouillon is fabulous for cooking vegetables because it adds so much flavor without adding calories.

BEEF CONSOMMÉ
(Clarified Beef Stock)

2 egg whites
4 cups defatted cold Beef Stock, page 24

Optional Ingredients
3 tablespoons lean ground beef
1/2 teaspoon chervil
1 parsley sprig

2 green onion tops, chopped
1 carrot, chopped
salt to taste

Makes 1 quart (4 cups)
Calories negligible

Whether you are serving consommé hot or cold, you will want it beautifully clear. The addition of egg whites clarifies it. Beat the egg whites with a wire whisk until they are slightly foamy. Add 1 cup of the cold stock to the egg whites and beat lightly together. Put the other 3 cups of stock in a very clean saucepan with all remaining ingredients. (It is not necessary to add the other ingredients, but the consommé will have a better flavor if you do.) Bring the stock to a boil and remove from the heat. Slowly pour the egg whites and stock mixture into the stock, stirring with the wire whisk as you do. Put the saucepan back on a very low heat and mix gently until it starts to simmer. Put the pan half on the heat and half off so that it is barely simmering, turning the pan around every few minutes. Simmer for 40 minutes.

Line a colander or a strainer with 2 or 3 layers of damp cheesecloth. Pour consommé into colander and let it drain undisturbed until it has all seeped through. Store until ready to use.

Variations If you are serving the consommé hot, just before serving add 2 tablespoons Madeira. If you are planning to serve the consommé cold and want it firm, or if you are going to use it for aspics or molded salads, add 2 tablespoons sherry and 1 scant tablespoon (1 envelope) unflavored gelatin dissolved in 1/4 cup cold water to every 2 cups of consommé while still hot.

soups

Because I love soups served both hot and cold, I have included recipes in this section which are equally good served either way. This will save you lots of time because the hot soup you make and serve for one meal can be stored in the refrigerator or freezer and served cold for another occasion.

Dress up your soup presentation when possible by serving it in unusual ways. Serve cold soups in icers, and hot soups in a variety of bowls or even mugs. Try serving my Cold Curried Grapefruit Soup in hollowed-out grapefruit halves and garnishing it with a sprig of mint.

WATERCRESS SOUP

6 cups chicken stock
1 onion
1 clove
1 celery stalk, without leaves
1 bay leaf
1 tablespoon unprocessed wheat bran
1/4 teaspoon thyme
1 cup chopped watercress

1/8 teaspoon white pepper
salt to taste

Makes 6 servings (4 cups)
Each serving contains approximately:
.4 gram of fiber
13 calories

Pour the chicken stock in a large saucepan or soup kettle. Stick the clove in the onion and add it to the chicken stock; add the celery, bay leaf, bran and thyme. Bring to a boil, reduce heat and simmer, covered, for 1-1/2 hours.

Remove the clove from the onion and the bay leaf and discard. Put all other ingredients in the saucepan in a blender and blend until smooth. Add the watercress, white pepper and salt and blend until the watercress is the desired size flecks in the soup.

Serve immediately or chill and serve cold. If reheated the watercress will lose its fresh, tangy flavor.

Variation This basic soup is good for all vegetables. I particularly like it for Vegetable Soup al Dente using a variety of steamed, crisp-tender vegetables in place of watercress. It is also good made with broccoli, cauliflower, asparagus, zucchini, carrots, green beans, peas—use your imagination!

soups

CHEDDAR CHEESE SOUP

1 tablespoon butter or corn oil margarine
2 tablespoons minced onion
1 large tomato, peeled, diced and mashed
1/4 cup whole wheat flour
4 cups low-fat milk, heated to the boiling point
1/2 teaspoon salt
1/4 teaspoon dry mustard
1/4 teaspoon sweet basil

1/2 teaspoon Worcestershire sauce
1/8 teaspoon white pepper
3 cups grated sharp cheddar cheese

Makes 6 servings (5 cups)
Each serving contains approximately:
.3 gram of fiber
276 calories

Melt the butter or margarine in a saucepan and add the minced onion. Cook for about 5 minutes, or until the onion is clear and tender. Add the tomato and flour and mix well. Bring mixture to a simmer and cook, stirring constantly, for 3 minutes. Remove from the heat and add half of the hot milk, stirring rapidly with a wire whisk until completely blended. Add the remaining milk and return to medium heat. Simmer slowly for 30 minutes, stirring frequently to prevent scorching. Add all other ingredients and continue cooking until the cheese is completely melted.

I often serve this soup with a big salad and Curried Corn Muffins for lunch or dinner.

Cheddar Cheese Sauce Variation Use 2 cups of milk instead of 4 cups and use this same recipe to make a delicious sauce. Cheddar Cheese Sauce is good on vegetables, eggs, fish, meat and poultry dishes, or try it on See's Soufflé-Squares. This recipe will make 3 cups of sauce; 1/4 cup contains approximately .1 gram of fiber and 118 calories.

ONION SOUP

1 tablespoon butter or corn oil margarine
3 medium onions, thinly sliced
4 cups beef stock
1/2 teaspoon salt
1/4 teaspoon freshly ground black pepper
4 teaspoons unprocessed wheat bran
1/4 cup grated Parmesan cheese

Makes 4 servings
Each serving contains approximately:
.6 gram of fiber
84 calories

Melt the butter or margarine in a large heavy iron skillet. Add the sliced onions and cook, covered, over very low heat, until onions are tender. Remove the lid and turn the heat up to high. Brown the onions, stirring constantly so that they don't burn. When they are brown, add 1 cup of the beef stock and cook until it is almost absorbed. Put the onion mixture in a large saucepan or soup kettle and add the remaining beef stock, salt, pepper and bran. Mix well and simmer for 5 minutes.

Divide the soup into 4 bowls and sprinkle 1 tablespoon of the Parmesan cheese over the top of each serving.

MARIANNE'S SIMPLE SPLIT PEA SOUP

1 pound split peas
8 cups (2 quarts) water
1 ham hock or ham bone
1 large onion, chopped
2 carrots, diced
2 large celery stalks, without leaves, chopped
1 bay leaf
1/2 teaspoon salt

3 cups chicken stock
sherry (optional)

Makes 11 cups
1 cup contains approximately:
2.3 grams of fiber
150 calories

Put all ingredients, except chicken stock and sherry, in a large soup kettle or stockpot. Bring to a boil. Reduce heat to very low, cover and cook for 5 to 6 hours. Cool to room temperature and refrigerate overnight.

When cold remove all visible fat from the top. Remove ham hock or bone and bay leaf. Put the skimmed soup in a blender, a little at a time, and purée. Pour puréed soup in a large pan and add the chicken stock. Heat well before serving. A teaspoon of sherry may be added to each bowl. Serve with Cheese Straws.

Last fall I spent three weeks in India with Dr. Leo Krall, the educational director of the Joslin Clinic, his wife, Lois and her sister Marianne Moss. While discussing soup one evening Marianne told us her favorite soup was split pea. This is my slightly lower calorie version of her delicious recipe.

soups

ORANGE SOUP

1 tablespoon hulled sesame seeds
8 or 9 large carrots, sliced (4 cups sliced)
1/2 cup chopped onion
2 cups chicken stock
1/2 teaspoon salt
4 tablespoons butter or corn oil margarine
1/4 cup whole wheat flour
4 cups low-fat milk,
   heated to the boiling point

1/4 teaspoon white pepper
1/2 teaspoon ground nutmeg
1 cup fresh orange juice

Makes 8 servings
Each serving contains approximately:
.2 gram of fiber
208 calories

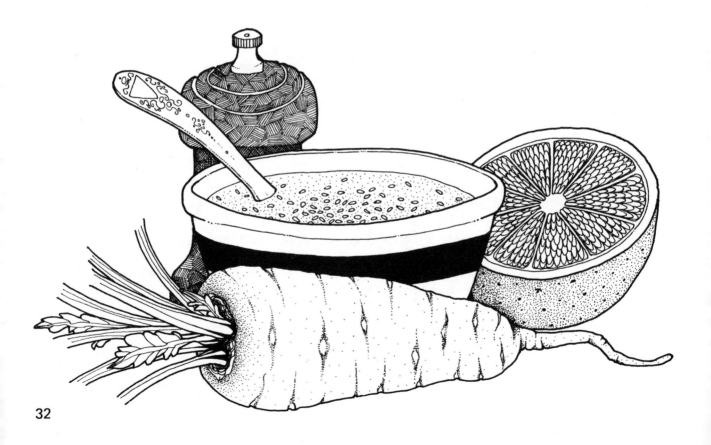

Preheat oven to 350°. Place the sesame seeds on a cookie sheet in the preheated oven for approximately 10 minutes or until a golden brown. Watch carefully as they burn easily. Set aside.

In a saucepan combine the carrots, onion, chicken stock and salt and bring to a boil. Reduce heat and simmer, covered, until carrots are tender, about 8 to 10 minutes.

While the carrots are cooking, melt the butter or margarine in another pan. Add the flour and cook, stirring, for 3 minutes. Remove from the heat and add the hot milk, all at once, stirring with a wire whisk. Put the milk mixture back on low heat and add the white pepper and nutmeg. Continue stirring occasionally for 10 to 15 minutes or until slightly thickened.

Put the cooked carrots and all their cooking liquid in a blender. Add the orange juice and blend until smooth. Pour the blended liquid into the saucepan with the other ingredients and mix well. Heat to desired temperature; *do not boil.*

Pour the soup into 8 bowls and sprinkle the toasted sesame seeds on top of each serving. If you have leftover soup, refrigerate it and serve it cold later in the week.

If your friends ask why you call this recipe "Orange Soup," ask them what color they would call it!

Variation Orange Soup is also good cold and it is beautiful served in icers.

PARSLEY SOUP

6 cups beef stock
1 onion
2 celery stalks, without leaves
1 bay leaf
1 cup chopped parsley
1/8 teaspoon white pepper

salt to taste

Makes 6 servings (4 cups)
Each serving contains approximately:
.3 gram of fiber
14 calories

Pour the beef stock in a large saucepan or soup kettle. Add the onion, celery and bay leaf to the beef stock. Bring to a boil, reduce heat and simmer, covered, for 1-1/2 hours.

Remove the bay leaf from the beef stock and discard. Put all other ingredients that are in the saucepan in a blender and blend until smooth. Add the parsley, white pepper and salt and blend until the parsley is the desired-size flecks in the soup.

Serve immediately or chill and serve cold. If reheated the parsley will lose its fresh flavor.

soups

LEEK AND BARLEY SOUP

1/2 cup pearl barley (1/4 pound)
2 tablespoons butter or corn oil margarine
4 leeks, white part only, chopped
2 garlic buds, chopped
8 cups chicken stock
1/8 teaspoon white pepper
salt to taste
2 cups buttermilk

1 tablespoon fresh lemon juice
1/2 cup finely chopped parsley

Makes 8 servings
Each serving contains approximately:
.1 gram of fiber
82 calories

Soak barley in water to cover for 2 hours, drain and set aside. Melt butter or margarine in a large skillet and cook leeks and garlic for 10 minutes. Do not brown. Combine cooked leeks, drained barley, chicken stock, pepper and salt in a soup kettle and simmer, covered, for 1-1/2 hours.

Combine 2 cups of the hot soup with the buttermilk. Mix well and return the mixture to the hot soup. Add the lemon juice and parsley to the soup, mix well and serve at once.

If you have leftover soup store it in the refrigerator and serve it cold the second time around. I like to put mine in the blender to make a smooth soup when served cold. If you prefer to reheat it be careful not to bring it to a boil. This is a hearty and unusual soup—hot or cold!

COLD BUTTERMILK BORSCHT

2 cups chopped, cold cooked beets
2 tablespoons unprocessed wheat bran
1 teaspoon garlic salt
1/8 teaspoon white pepper
1/2 teaspoon ground allspice
1/2 cup sour cream
2 cups buttermilk

1/4 cup non-fat plain yogurt
1 tablespoon minced parsley

Makes 4 servings
Each serving contains approximately:
1.0 gram of fiber
175 calories

Combine all ingredients, except yogurt and parsley, in a blender and blend until smooth. Serve in chilled bowls or icers. Put 1 tablespoon of yogurt and a sprinkle of minced parsley on the top of each serving.

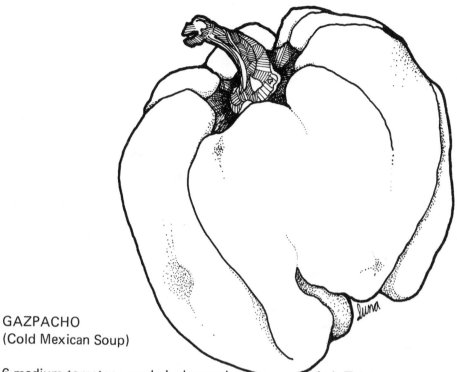

GAZPACHO
(Cold Mexican Soup)

6 medium tomatoes, peeled, chopped
  and mashed (4 cups)
1 medium onion, chopped
1 small green chili, seeded and
  chopped (1 tablespoon)
1 medium cucumber, chopped
1 small green bell pepper, seeded and chopped
1-1/2 teaspoons Worcestershire sauce
1 garlic bud, chopped
2 teaspoons seasoned salt

dash Tabasco sauce
1/4 teaspoon freshly ground black pepper
1 large tomato, finely diced (1 cup)
1/4 cup finely chopped chives
  or green onion tops
2 lemons, cut in wedges

Makes 8 servings
Each serving contains approximately:
1.2 grams of fiber
43 calories

Put half of the mashed tomatoes into the blender and all other ingredients, except the diced tomatoes, chives and lemon wedges. Blend until well mixed. Slowly add the remaining mashed tomatoes to the blender and blend. Chill.

Pour the mixture into a large bowl and add the diced tomatoes. Garnish with the chopped chives and serve with the lemon wedges.

I usually serve this with Toasted Tortilla Triangles, or for a change serve with Cheese Straws.   35

WATERMELON SOUP

5 cups seeded and diced ripe watermelon pulp
2 teaspoons unprocessed wheat bran
salt to taste (If you like salt on
   watermelon you will like a little salt
   in this soup—if not, you won't!)
fresh mint for garnish (optional)

Makes 4 servings
Each serving contains approximately:
.9 gram of fiber
67 calories

Put 4 cups of the diced watermelon in a blender. Set aside the remaining 1 cup of diced watermelon to add later. Add the bran and salt to the blender and blend until smooth. Pour the soup into 4 chilled bowls or icers. Add 1/4 cup of the remaining diced watermelon to each serving. Garnish each serving with a sprig of fresh mint.

COLD CURRIED GRAPEFRUIT SOUP

4 cups fresh grapefruit juice, unstrained
3 tablespoons quick-cooking tapioca
1/4 teaspoon salt
1 teaspoon date "sugar"
1/2 teaspoon curry powder
6 tablespoons non-fat plain yogurt

2 tablespoons Toasted Bran Flakes, page 51

Makes 6 servings
Each serving contains approximately:
.2 gram of fiber
66 calories

Combine all ingredients, except the sour cream and Toasted Bran Flakes, in a saucepan. Allow to stand for 5 minutes. Put the pan on medium heat and bring to a boil, stirring frequently. As soon as it comes to a boil, remove the pan from the heat and cool to room temperature. Cover and refrigerate until cold. Serve in chilled bowls or hollowed-out grapefruit halves. Stir 1 tablespoon of yogurt and 1 teaspoon Toasted Bran Flakes lightly through each serving.

This is a delightfully different first course for a brunch menu. I like to serve it with Green Eggs and Ham en Croustade.

STRAWBERRY SOUP

3 cups sliced strawberries
1 cup fresh orange juice
1 tablespoon unprocessed wheat bran
1 tablespoon date "sugar"
1/2 teaspoon vanilla extract

Makes 4 servings
Each serving contains approximately:
2 grams of fiber
75 calories

Put 2 cups of the sliced strawberries in a blender. Set the remaining cup of sliced strawberries aside to add later. Add all of the other ingredients to the blender and blend until smooth. Pour the soup into 4 bowls and add 1/4 cup of the remaining sliced strawberries to each bowl.

This is a lovely, light soup to serve before a luncheon or it goes very well with poultry, ham or pork dinners.

sauces, gravies and toppings

Just a few fibrous sauces will solve all your problems concerning the addition of fiber to fiberless proteins such as eggs, fish, poultry and meat and add variety to your menus.

Try serving a broiled meat patty covered with Onion Sauce, baked fish with Fresh Dill Sauce or sliced turkey with Curried Cranberry Sauce and you will see what I mean. Variety is truly the "spice of life," and sauces offer that necessary "spice" to the daily diet.

DEFATTED DRIPPINGS

If you love gravy but don't eat it because it's fat, fat, fat, then one of your problems can be solved. Just defat your drippings. All drippings are defatted in the same manner. After cooking your roast beef, leg of lamb, chicken, turkey or whatever, remove it from the roasting pan and pour the drippings into a bowl. Put the bowl in the refrigerator until the drippings are cold and all of the fat has solidified on the top. Remove the fat and you have defatted drippings.

Now, if you are in a hurry for them because you want to serve your roast beef au jus with defatted drippings instead of "fat jus," then put the drippings in the freezer instead of the refrigerator. Put the roast in a warm oven to keep it from getting cold. After about 20 minutes you can remove the fat, heat the jus and serve. I always defat my drippings when I roast meat or poultry and then keep them in the freezer. Defatted drippings add extra flavor to your stocks and are better than stocks for making the following High-Low Gravies, high in fiber and low in calories. The calories in defatted drippings are negligible.

sauces, gravies and toppings

HIGH-LOW BEEF GRAVY
(High in Fiber—Low in Calories)

1 cup Defatted Beef Drippings, page 39
1 cup beef stock
2 tablespoons cornstarch or arrowroot
1 tablespoon unprocessed wheat bran
1/4 cup water
salt

Makes 1 to 1-1/2 cups
1/4 cup contains approximately:
.1 gram of fiber
13 calories

Heat the Defatted Beef Drippings and beef stock in a saucepan. Mix the cornstarch or arrowroot and bran with the water and add to the gravy. Cook over medium heat, stirring occasionally, until thickened. Add salt to taste.

HIGH-LOW TURKEY MUSHROOM GRAVY
(High in Fiber—Low in Calories)

2 cups Defatted Turkey Drippings, page 39
2 cups beef stock
3 tablespoons cornstarch or arrowroot
1 tablespoon unprocessed wheat bran
1/4 cup water
2 teaspoons butter or corn oil margarine
1/2 cup sliced mushrooms

salt and freshly ground black pepper

Makes 2 to 3 cups
1/4 cup contains approximately:
.1 gram of fiber
9 calories

Heat the Defatted Turkey Drippings and beef stock in a saucepan. Mix the cornstarch or arrowroot and bran with the water and add to the gravy. Cook slowly over medium heat, stirring occasionally, until mixture thickens slightly. While the gravy is cooking, heat the butter or margarine in a skillet and add the sliced mushrooms. Cook until tender and add to the gravy. Season to taste with salt and pepper.

BROWN-BRAN SAUCE

1/2 cup unprocessed wheat bran
1/2 cup burgundy
1/4 cup sherry
1/4 cup chablis
1 tablespoon finely chopped shallots or
green onion tops
4 cups beef stock, heated
1/4 cup cornstarch
1/4 cup water

1/2 teaspoon salt
1/8 teaspoon freshly ground black pepper
2 teaspoons Kitchen Bouquet

Makes about 4 cups
1/2 cup contains approximately:
.6 gram of fiber
40 calories

Preheat the oven to 350°. Put the bran in an 8- or 9-inch cake pan. Place the cake pan in the center of the preheated oven for approximately 10 minutes, or until the bran is well toasted. Every 3 or 4 minutes shake the pan so that the bran will toast evenly. Watch them carefully because they burn easily and quickly!

In a large saucepan, combine the 3 wines, shallots or green onion tops and toasted bran. Cook over fairly high heat, boiling mixture until it has reduced one-third in volume. When it has reduced, add the hot beef stock to the wine and lower the heat to medium.

Mix the cornstarch and water until cornstarch is completely dissolved. When the wine mixture has again come to a simmering boil, add the cornstarch mixture, mixing thoroughly using a wire whisk. Add the salt, pepper and Kitchen Bouquet and mix until well blended.

Using this sauce is a marvelous way to add fiber to otherwise fiberless meat and poultry. Use it as you would use a basic brown sauce.

sauces, gravies and toppings

MUSHROOM SAUCE

3 tablespoons butter or corn oil margarine
1 pound mushrooms, sliced
4 cups Brown-Bran Sauce, page 41, heated

Makes about 5 cups
1/4 cup contains approximately:
.4 gram of fiber
40 calories

Melt the butter or margarine in a skillet. Add the mushrooms and cook until just tender. Do not overcook the mushrooms, as they will reduce too much in volume because they contain so much moisture. Pour the heated Brown-Bran Sauce into a large skillet with the mushrooms, mix thoroughly and heat through.

This sauce is so good, it makes any simple dish, such as scrambled eggs, ground meat patties or any leftover meat, chicken, fish, vegetables, a gourmet delight.

Variation Substitute Not Quite White Sauce for Brown-Bran Sauce.

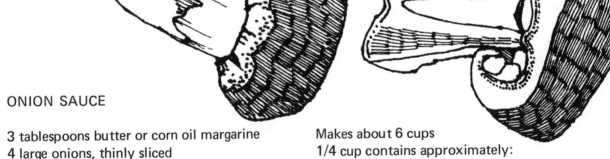
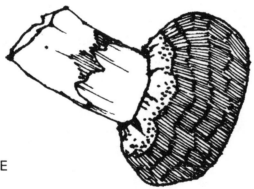

ONION SAUCE

3 tablespoons butter or corn oil margarine
4 large onions, thinly sliced
4 cups Brown-Bran Sauce, page 41, heated

Makes about 6 cups
1/4 cup contains approximately:
.6 gram of fiber
35 calories

Melt the butter or margarine in a large skillet. Add the sliced onions and cook until the onions are lightly browned. Pour the Brown-Bran Sauce into the skillet with the onions and mix thoroughly. This sauce, like the Mushroom Sauce, is good served with almost anything!

42   *Variation* Substitute Not Quite White Sauce for Brown-Bran Sauce.

TOMATO SAUCE

1 tablespoon corn oil
1/2 medium onion, minced
2 garlic buds, minced
1/4 teaspoon thyme
1 bay leaf
6 medium tomatoes, peeled and diced
1 teaspoon salt

1/4 teaspoon freshly ground black pepper
2 tablespoons unprocessed wheat bran

Makes about 3-1/2 cups
1/2 cup contains approximately:
.8 gram of fiber
47 calories

Heat the oil in a large saucepan with a lid. Add the onion, garlic, thyme and bay leaf. Cover and cook 5 to 10 minutes over low heat or until onion is tender. Add the diced tomatoes, salt, pepper and bran and mix well. Cover and continue to cook on low heat for 10 minutes. Pour contents of pan into a blender and blend until smooth.

This is a good basic tomato sauce for vegetables, eggs, fish, poultry and meat and can be used in many of the recipes in this book.

CHILI SAUCE

12 ripe tomatoes, chopped and mashed (8 cups)
1 medium onion, finely chopped
1 large green bell pepper, finely chopped
1 garlic bud, minced
3/4 cup date "sugar"
1/4 cup unprocessed wheat bran
1-1/2 tablespoons salt
1 tablespoon pickling spices

1-1/2 teaspoons mustard seed
1/2 teaspoon celery seed
3/4 cup cider vinegar

Makes about 7 cups
1 cup contains approximately:
3 grams of fiber
142 calories

Combine tomatoes, onion, bell pepper, garlic, date "sugar," bran and salt in a large saucepan. Bring to a boil, reduce heat and simmer, uncovered, for 45 minutes. Remove 1 cup of the sauce and put it in a blender. Add the pickling spices, mustard seed and celery seed and blend until smooth. Pour the contents of the blender back into the pan. Add the vinegar and continue to cook, stirring frequently, for another 45 minutes or until the sauce is quite thick.

sauces, gravies and toppings

FRESH DILL SAUCE

2 tablespoons cider vinegar
2 tablespoons corn oil
1 teaspoon date "sugar"
1 tablespoon chopped parsley
1 tablespoon chopped chives or green
   onion tops
3 tablespoons chopped fresh dill
   (or 2 teaspoons dillweed)
1/4 teaspoon white pepper
1/2 teaspoon salt

1 cup chopped watercress leaves
1 garlic bud, chopped
2 tablespoons fresh lemon juice
1/2 cup mayonnaise

Makes 1-1/4 cups
1/4 cup contains approximately:
.3 gram of fiber
283 calories

Combine all ingredients, except mayonnaise, in a blender and blend until smooth. Pour blended ingredients into a mixing bowl, add the mayonnaise and mix well with a wire whisk. This is not only a deliciously different salad dressing, it is also a superb sauce on all types of fish and seafood. I also like it on cold chicken and turkey.

CURRY-CHEESE SAUCE
(For vegetable sauce or a dip)

1 cup Creamy Curry Dressing, page 58
1/4 teaspoon curry powder (optional; if you
   prefer a stronger curry flavor)
1/2 cup ricotta cheese

Makes 1-1/2 cups
1/4 cup contains approximately:
.2 gram of fiber
233 calories

Mix all ingredients well using a pastry blender. Do not blend in an electric blender or the sauce will not be thick enough to serve as a "non-drip" dip! Store in the refrigerator in a jar with a tight-fitting lid.

   Always try to prepare this sauce at least 24 hours before you plan to use it because the flavor will be greatly improved.

CHEDDAR CHEESE SAUCE

See Cheddar Cheese Sauce Variation on page 30.

FRESH MINT SAUCE

1/2 cup minced fresh mint leaves
3 tablespoons date "sugar"
1 cup white wine vinegar

Makes about 1 cup
2 tablespoons contain approximately:
.2 gram of fiber
16 calories

To prepare the mint, wash and thoroughly dry the leaves, then mince them as fine as coarsely ground pepper. (It is impossible to mince damp mint leaves finely enough.) Put the minced mint in a non-metal bowl. Add the date "sugar" and mix well. Pour the white wine vinegar over the mint mixture and allow it to stand for at least 3 hours at room temperature before serving.

   Make only the amount of sauce you plan to use because it loses the fresh mint flavor if stored in the refrigerator. Try Fresh Mint Sauce instead of mint jelly with lamb. It contains fewer calories, more fiber, and, I think, it tastes better.

45

sauces, gravies and toppings

FLORENTINE SAUCE

2 pounds spinach
2 tablespoons butter or corn oil margarine
3 tablespoons whole wheat flour
2 cups low-fat milk
1 teaspoon salt
1-3/4 cups ricotta cheese
1/4 cup grated Romano cheese

1/2 teaspoon oregano
1/4 teaspoon ground nutmeg

Makes about 6 cups
1 cup contains approximately:
1.5 grams of fiber
254 calories

Carefully wash spinach and break off the tough ends. Chop spinach. Steam the chopped spinach for about 2 to 3 minutes and drain well, pressing through a sieve to make sure all water is removed. Set aside.

In the top of a double boiler placed over boiling water, melt the butter or margarine and add flour, stirring constantly for about 3 minutes. Add the milk, a little at a time, stirring constantly with a wire whisk. Add the salt and continue to stir until sauce thickens, about 10 minutes. Add all other ingredients, including drained spinach, mix thoroughly and heat through.

This is my favorite sauce for a variety of Italian entrées. It may also be served as a side dish with meat, poultry, fish or seafood.

CURRIED CRANBERRY SAUCE

1 cup fresh orange juice
1 cup date "sugar"
4 cups (1 pound) fresh cranberries
3 medium oranges, peeled and diced
1 cup raisins
1 teaspoon salt
1 teaspoon curry powder

1/4 teaspoon ground ginger

Makes about 4-1/2 cups
1/4 cup contains approximately:
.9 gram of fiber
87 calories

Combine orange juice, date "sugar" and cranberries in a large saucepan and bring to a boil. Reduce heat, cover and simmer for 15 minutes. Add all other ingredients and simmer uncovered for 10 to 15 minutes, stirring occasionally. Cool to room temperature and refrigerate in a tightly covered container for at least 24 hours before serving.

This is a delightfully different cranberry sauce to serve with your traditional holiday meals.

JELLED MILK

1/4 cup water
1 scant tablespoon (1 envelope) unflavored
   gelatin
1 cup milk (non-fat, low-fat or buttermilk)

Makes 1 cup
1 cup contains approximately:
80 calories (non-fat or buttermilk)
125 calories (low-fat milk)

Put the water in a small saucepan. Sprinkle the gelatin on the top and allow it to soften for 5 minutes. Place the saucepan on low heat, stirring constantly, until the gelatin is completely dissolved. Do not allow it to come to a boil. Slowly pour the milk into the gelatin, stirring as you do. Place the gelatin-milk mixture, covered, in the refrigerator. When it is jelled, it is ready to use as Jelled Milk for many recipes. I even prefer equal portions of plain cold milk and Jelled Milk mixed in the blender and then poured over fruit or breakfast cereal to just plain milk. It makes the dish seem so much richer.

NOT QUITE WHITE SAUCE

2 tablespoons butter or corn oil margarine
3 tablespoons whole wheat flour
2 cups low-fat milk, heated to the boiling point
1 teaspoon salt

Makes about 2 cups
1/4 cup contains approximately:
trace of fiber
74 calories

In the top of a double boiler placed over boiling water, melt the butter or margarine and add flour. Cook, stirring constantly, for about 3 minutes. Add the milk, a little at a time, stirring constantly with a wire whisk. Add the salt and continue to stir until sauce thickens, about 10 minutes. If you want a thicker sauce, continue cooking and stirring until sauce is the desired consistency.

sauces, gravies and toppings

DATE "SUGAR"

36 dates, pitted and sliced

Makes 1 cup

1 tablespoon contains approximately:
.5 gram of fiber
40 calories

Spread pitted, sliced dates evenly over an ungreased cookie sheet, being careful not to overlap them. Put the dates in a 250° oven for about 12 to 15 hours, or until they are completely dried out and hard. Dates contain different amounts of moisture, so cooking time will vary. Watch carefully that they do not burn. Turn the oven off, leave the door open slightly and cool the dates to room temperature.

Put the hard dates (and they will be *very* hard—like rocks!) in the blender. Turn the blender on and add the hard dates, a few at a time, until they have all been reduced to a powdery, sugar-like substance.

It is easier by far to buy date "sugar" at your local natural foods store, but if you can't find it, or just want to know how it is made, I have included the method for you. I use date "sugar" in many of my recipes in the book for sweetening because it is a pure food and can be used by diabetics and others on sugar-restricted diets.

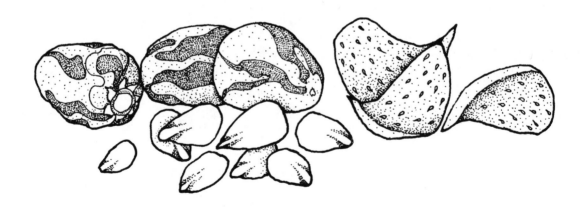

DATE BUTTER

1 cup date "sugar"
3/4 cup water
4 tablespoons butter or corn oil
　　at room temperature
1 teaspoon vanilla extract

Makes about 1-1/4 cups
1 tablespoon contains approximately:
.4 gram of fiber
63 calories

Combine date "sugar" and water in a saucepan. Bring to a boil over medium heat. Reduce heat and simmer, uncovered, for 20 minutes or until all water is absorbed. Remove from heat and cool to room temperature. Combine all ingredients in a bowl and using a pastry blender, mix until a smooth consistency. Store in the refrigerator in a covered container.

　　Use Date Butter just as you would use jam or honey, and for a real treat try a Hot Date Butter Sundae.

DATE SYRUP

1 cup date "sugar"
2 cups water
1 teaspoon vanilla extract
1/4 teaspoon ground cinnamon

Makes about 1-3/4 cups
2 tablespoons contain approximately:
.5 gram of fiber
51 calories

Combine all ingredients in a saucepan and bring to a boil. Reduce heat to medium-low and simmer, stirring frequently, for 1 hour. Cool to room temperature, put in a blender and blend until smooth. Store in the refrigerator; heat slightly before using on anything you are serving hot.

　　Use Date Syrup just as you would use maple syrup on pancakes, waffles, French toast, ice cream, even chicken and fish! It is higher in fiber and lower in calories than maple syrup or honey.

sauces, gravies and toppings

BERRY-BRAN JAM OR SAUCE

2 cups fresh whole berries (strawberries, raspberries, blackberries, boysenberries or blueberries)
1/4 cup date "sugar"
1 teaspoon unflavored gelatin
1 teaspoon fresh lemon juice

2 teaspoons unprocessed wheat bran

Makes about 2 cups
1/2 cup contains approximately:
1.6 grams of fiber
75 calories

Combine the berries and date "sugar" in a saucepan with a tight-fitting lid. Cook, covered, over very low heat for about 10 minutes. Remove the lid and bring the juice to a boil. Boil for 1 minute and remove from the heat. Soften the gelatin in the lemon juice. Pour the hot berry juice into the softened gelatin and stir until gelatin is completely dissolved. Add the dissolved gelatin to the berries. Add the bran and mix well. Allow to cool to room temperature and store in the refrigerator.

This jam is good all by itself! It is also great used as you would any other jam or as a sauce on ice cream. For a super breakfast try a Berry-Bran Jam omelet.

SHERRIED FRUIT TOPPING

2 tablespoons butter or corn oil margarine
2 cups peeled and thinly sliced fresh fruit
(I like peaches best, but when they are not in season I use apples or pears.)
1/4 cup date "sugar"
1/8 teaspoon salt

1/2 cup sherry

Makes 2 cups
1/4 cup contains approximately:
.6 gram of fiber
68 calories

Melt butter or margarine in a skillet. Add all other ingredients and mix thoroughly. Cook over medium-low heat, stirring frequently, about 20 minutes or until fruit is tender and most of the liquid is absorbed.

This topping is fabulous on Super Baked Pancakes. It is also delicious on French toast, Wheat Germ Waffles, ice cream—use your imagination.

TOASTED BRAN FLAKES

1 cup unprocessed wheat bran

Makes 1 cup

1 tablespoon contains approximately:
.6 gram of fiber
13 calories

Preheat oven to 350°. Put the bran in an 8- or 9-inch cake pan. Place the cake pan in the center of the preheated oven for approximately 10 minutes, or until well toasted. Every 3 or 4 minutes shake the pan so that the bran flakes will toast evenly. Watch them carefully because they burn easily *and* quickly!

I like my bran flakes better toasted on fruits and on other cereals, and they are good sprinkled on salads.

TOASTED ALMOND FLAKES

shelled almonds (the quantity depends on
    the amount of almond flakes you want
    to make)
salt

7 almonds make 1 tablespoon
1 tablespoon contains approximately:
.3 gram of fiber
65 calories

Preheat the oven to 350°. Place almonds on a cutting board and mince with a sharp knife, as you would parsley or chives. Do not put them in the blender because often you will be using so few almonds you will turn them into dust rather than the desired flaky texture. Place the almond flakes on a cookie sheet and lightly salt them. Place in the preheated oven for about 10 minutes, watching carefully because they burn quickly. Toast them to the desired brownness. (I like mine very toasted.)

The advantage of using Toasted Almond Flakes in recipes instead of sliced or chopped almonds is that they are light in texture and can be sprinkled like snowflakes onto salads, entrées or desserts. It also requires fewer almonds to get the same amount of flavor, thereby cutting the calories down tremendously. Toasted Almond Flakes should not be prepared ahead and stored, because they will lose a great deal of their flavor.

salads and salad dressings

Salads are my favorite form of food. They offer variety to menu planning, and when you use my fabulous fiber salad dressings, they also contribute an adequate amount of fiber for most meals.

The salad dressing can truly "make or break" the salad. Even as much as I love salad, I have been served dressings I disliked so much I didn't enjoy the salad. Too much dressing can turn a bowl of crisp, beautiful greens into a sad, soggy mess.

The dressing recipes in this chapter are unique in that each dressing contains fiber. One usually thinks of the dietary fiber all being found in the salad itself and only the calories in the dressing. My dressings offer you not only a high fiber content but also a wide variety in flavor range and calorie content. Try my Fabulous Mayonnaise—it has only one-half the calories found in most mayonnaise and fiber too!

A high-fiber, low-calorie salad can be a side dish, a separate course served before or after the entrée or it can be the entrée itself. My own favorite luncheon is Jeanne Appleseed Salad. That's why I stole Johnny's name and use my own!

Always try to wash salad greens several hours before you plan to serve them. Pat them dry and then place them in a colander so that any remaining moisture will drip through. Place the colander on a plate to catch the water and refrigerate until ready to use. Not only will your salads be crisper when the lettuce or other salad greens are completely dry, but you will need far less salad dressing to completely coat each leaf. Using less dressing makes a big difference in the total number of calories per serving of salad, so to lower the calorie count *dry those greens.*

Chill your salad plates in the freezer. Salads should always be served on very cold plates.

salads and salad dressings

FABULOUS MAYONNAISE

2 tablespoons cornstarch
3 tablespoons red wine vinegar
1 cup water, boiling
1 egg, dipped in boiling water for 30 seconds
1/4 cup unprocessed wheat bran
1 teaspoon date "sugar"
1 teaspoon dry mustard
1 teaspoon salt

dash Tabasco sauce
1 cup corn oil

Makes 2 cups
2 tablespoons contain approximately:
.2 gram of fiber
148 calories

Combine cornstarch and vinegar in a saucepan. Stir in boiling water, using a wire whisk. Cook over low heat, stirring occasionally, until thickened and translucent, about 12 minutes. Pour the cornstarch mixture into a blender. Add the egg, bran, date "sugar," dry mustard, salt and Tabasco sauce. Blend until well mixed. Slowly add the oil, blending until smooth. Pour the mixture into a jar with a tight-fitting lid and store in the refrigerator.

I use this dressing warm over chicken, meat and fish. I serve it as a dip as well as for salad dressing. It is an excellent way to add fiber content to meat and other low fiber foods.

Fabulous Lemon Mayonnaise Variation Substitute 3 tablespoons of fresh lemon juice for the red wine vinegar and proceed exactly as you do for Fabulous Mayonnaise.

FABULOUS MAYONNAISE DRESSING AND DIP

1 cup Fabulous Mayonnaise, preceding
1/2 teaspoon brown mustard
1/4 teaspoon Worcestershire sauce
1/4 teaspoon soy sauce
1 garlic bud, crushed

Makes 1-1/2 cups
2 tablespoons contain approximately:
.1 gram of fiber
98 calories

Mix all ingredients well and store in the refrigerator in a jar with a tight-fitting lid. Always try to prepare this dip at least 24 hours before you plan to use it because the flavor will be greatly improved.

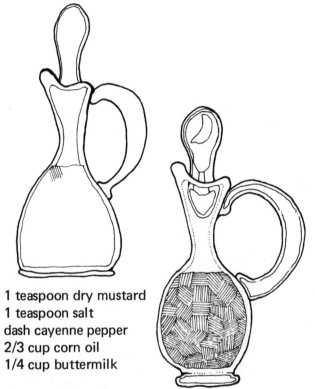

GREEN GODDESS DRESSING

2 tablespoons cornstarch
1/4 cup tarragon vinegar
1 cup water, boiling
1 egg, dipped in boiling water for 30 seconds
5 anchovy fillets, drained and chopped
1/4 cup unprocessed wheat bran
1/2 cup minced or chopped parsley
1/4 cup chopped green onions
1/2 garlic bud, chopped
1 tablespoon date "sugar"

1 teaspoon dry mustard
1 teaspoon salt
dash cayenne pepper
2/3 cup corn oil
1/4 cup buttermilk

Makes 3-1/4 cups
2 tablespoons contain approximately:
.1 gram of fiber
45 calories

Combine cornstarch and vinegar in saucepan. Stir in boiling water, using a wire whisk. Cook over low heat, stirring occasionally, until thickened and translucent, about 12 minutes. Pour the cornstarch mixture into a blender. Add the egg, anchovy fillets, bran, parsley, green onions, garlic, date "sugar," mustard, salt and cayenne pepper. Blend until well mixed. Slowly add the oil, blending until smooth. Pour the mixture into a large mixing bowl and slowly add the buttermilk, stirring with a wire whisk. Mix until well blended. Store in the refrigerator in a jar with a tight-fitting lid.

salads and salad dressings

CREAMY BLUE CHEESE DRESSING

2 tablespoons cornstarch
1/4 cup red wine vinegar
1 cup water, boiling
1 egg, dipped in boiling water for 30 seconds
1 garlic bud, chopped
1/4 cup unprocessed wheat bran
1 tablespoon date "sugar"
1 teaspoon dry mustard
1 teaspoon salt
1/4 teaspoon Worcestershire sauce

dash Tabasco sauce
1-1/2 cups crumbled blue cheese (6 ounces)
3/4 cup corn oil
1/2 cup buttermilk

Makes 3 cups
2 tablespoons contain approximately:
.1 gram of fiber
103 calories

Combine the cornstarch and vinegar in a saucepan. Stir in boiling water, using a wire whisk. Cook over low heat, stirring occasionally until thickened and translucent, about 12 minutes. Pour the cornstarch mixture into a blender. Add the egg, garlic, bran, date "sugar," mustard, salt, Worcestershire sauce, Tabasco and blue cheese and blend until well mixed. Slowly add the oil, blending until smooth. Pour the mixture into a large mixing bowl and slowly add the buttermilk, mixing with a wire whisk until well blended. Store refrigerated in a jar with a tight-fitting lid.

1000 ISLAND DRESSING

2 tablespoons cornstarch
3 tablespoons fresh lemon juice
1 cup water, boiling
1 egg, dipped in boiling water for 30 seconds
1 teaspoon date "sugar"
1 teaspoon dry mustard
1 teaspoon salt
1/8 teaspoon freshly ground black pepper
1/4 cup chili sauce
1 tablespoon chopped onion

1/2 garlic bud, chopped
1/2 cup corn oil
1/4 cup chopped chives or green onion tops
2 tablespoons chopped green bell pepper
1 tablespoon chopped pimiento

Makes 2-1/2 cups
2 tablespoons contain approximately:
.1 gram of fiber
70 calories

Combine cornstarch and lemon juice in a saucepan. Stir in boiling water, using a wire whisk. Cook over low heat, stirring occasionally until thickened and translucent, about 12 minutes. Pour the cornstarch mixture into a blender. Add the egg, date "sugar," mustard, salt, pepper, chili sauce, chopped onion and garlic. Blend until well mixed. Slowly add the oil, blending until smooth. Pour the mixture into another container. Add the chopped chives, bell pepper and pimiento and mix well. Pour into a jar with a tight-fitting lid. Store in the refrigerator.

salads and salad dressings

CREAMY CURRY DRESSING

2 tablespoons cornstarch
1/4 cup fresh lemon juice
1 cup water, boiling
1 egg, dipped in boiling water for 30 seconds
1/4 cup unprocessed wheat bran
2 teaspoons date "sugar"
1/2 teaspoon dry mustard
1/2 teaspoon curry powder
1/8 teaspoon ground ginger

1/2 teaspoon salt
dash cayenne pepper
1 cup corn oil

Makes 2 cups
2 tablespoons contain approximately:
.2 gram of fiber
156 calories

Combine cornstarch and lemon juice in a saucepan. Stir in boiling water, using a wire whisk. Cook over low heat, stirring occasionally until thickened and translucent, about 12 minutes. Pour the cornstarch mixture into a blender. Add the egg, bran, date "sugar," dry mustard, curry powder, ginger, salt and cayenne pepper. Blend until well mixed. Slowly add the oil, blending until smooth. Store in the refrigerator in a jar with a tight-fitting lid.

GORGONZOLA CHEESE DRESSING

1-1/2 cups buttermilk
1/4 cup red wine vinegar
2 tablespoons corn oil
2 teaspoons seasoned salt
2 garlic buds, chopped
1/4 cup unprocessed wheat bran
dash Tabasco sauce

1-1/2 cups crumbled gorgonzola cheese
  (6 ounces)

Makes 2-1/2 cups
2 tablespoons contain approximately:
.1 gram of fiber
45 calories

Put all ingredients except gorgonzola cheese into a blender and blend until smooth. Put the gorgonzola cheese in a bowl and mash it well. Pour the contents of the blender over the cheese and mix together until a creamy consistency. Store refrigerated in a jar with a tight-fitting lid.

I try to make this dressing the day before I want to use it because the flavor improves. In fact, I try to keep a jar of it in the refrigerator all the time; it is my family's favorite dressing.

FRENCH FIBER DRESSING

1-1/2 teaspoons salt
1/4 cup red wine vinegar
1 teaspoon date "sugar"
1/4 teaspoon freshly ground black pepper
1-1/2 teaspoons fresh lemon juice
3/4 teaspoon Worcestershire sauce
1/2 teaspoon Dijon-style mustard
1/2 garlic bud, crushed

1/4 cup water
1/4 cup unprocessed wheat bran
1 cup corn oil

Makes 1-1/2 cups
2 tablespoons contain approximately:
.2 gram of fiber
186 calories

Dissolve salt in the vinegar. Add all other ingredients except oil and mix well, then slowly stir in the oil. Pour into a jar with a tight-fitting lid and shake vigorously for a full minute. Store tightly covered in the refrigerator.

ITALIAN FIBER DRESSING

1-1/2 teaspoons salt
1/4 cup red wine vinegar
1/4 cup dry red wine
1/2 teaspoon date "sugar"
1/2 teaspoon oregano
1/4 teaspoon sweet basil
1/4 teaspoon tarragon
1/2 teaspoon dry mustard
1/4 teaspoon freshly ground black pepper

3/4 teaspoon Worcestershire sauce
1 garlic bud, crushed
1/4 cup unprocessed wheat bran
1/2 cup corn oil

Makes 1-1/2 cups
2 tablespoons contain approximately:
.2 gram of fiber
96 calories

Dissolve salt in the vinegar and red wine. Add all other ingredients, except corn oil, and mix well, then slowly stir in the oil. Pour in a jar with a tight-fitting lid and shake vigorously for a full minute. Store tightly covered in the refrigerator.

salads and salad dressings

MEXICAN FIBER DRESSING

1-1/2 teaspoons salt
1/4 cup red wine vinegar
1 teaspoon date "sugar"
1/4 teaspoon freshly ground black pepper
1-1/2 teaspoons fresh lemon juice
3/4 teaspoon Worcestershire sauce
1/2 teaspoon chili powder
1/2 teaspoon dry mustard
1/2 teaspoon ground cumin
1/4 teaspoon oregano

1/2 garlic bud, minced
1/4 cup water
1/4 cup unprocessed wheat bran
dash Tabasco sauce
1 cup corn oil

Makes 1-1/2 cups
2 tablespoons contain approximately:
.2 gram of fiber
186 calories

Dissolve salt in the vinegar. Add all other ingredients except corn oil and mix well, then slowly stir in oil. Pour in a jar with a tight-fitting lid and shake vigorously for a full minute. Store tightly covered in the refrigerator.

LEMON-PEPPER DRESSING

1 teaspoon salt
1/3 cup fresh lemon juice
1 teaspoon freshly ground black pepper
1 teaspoon Worcestershire sauce
3/4 cup sesame oil
1/4 cup unprocessed wheat bran

Makes 1-1/2 cups
2 tablespoons contain approximately:
.2 gram of fiber
141 calories

Mix the salt in the lemon juice until completely dissolved. Add all other ingredients and mix well. Store tightly covered in the refrigerator. Use Lemon-Pepper Dressing sparingly as a little goes a long way! This dressing is also an excellent sauce for meat and poultry and can be used as a barbecue marinade.

LEMON-CHEESE DRESSING

1 teaspoon salt
1/4 cup fresh lemon juice
1/2 teaspoon freshly ground black pepper
3/4 cup corn oil
3/4 cup grated Parmesan cheese
1/4 cup unprocessed wheat bran

Makes 2 cups
2 tablespoons contain approximately:
.1 gram of fiber
118 calories

Mix the salt in the lemon juice until dissolved. Add all other ingredients and mix well. This is a very strong dressing and very little is needed on each serving. This is an advantage because the less dressing used on each salad the fewer calories you are adding! Store tightly covered in the refrigerator.

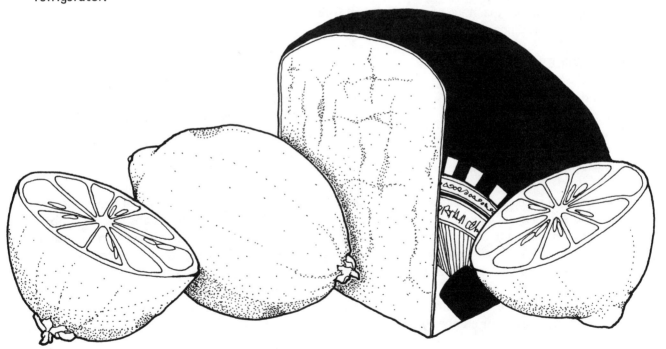

salads and salad dressings

FRUIT SALAD DRESSING

1/2 cup unsweetened pineapple juice
1 tablespoon champagne vinegar
1 tablespoon dry white wine
1 tablespoon soy sauce
1 tablespoon date "sugar"
2 tablespoons unsweetened shredded coconut
2 tablespoons unprocessed wheat bran

1/4 teaspoon coconut extract
1/2 cup corn oil

Makes 1-1/2 cups
2 tablespoons contain approximately:
.3 gram of fiber
112 calories

Combine all ingredients except corn oil and shake well in a jar with a tight-fitting lid. Add the oil and shake for 30 seconds. Chill before using.

This is an excellent dressing for fresh fruit salads. However, the reason I call it Fruit Salad Dressing is because it is made of practically all fruit ingredients. It is equally good on other salads and a marvelous sauce on barbecue chicken.

DATE-CHEESE DRESSING

1 cup date "sugar"
3/4 cup water
1 cup ricotta cheese (or low-fat cottage cheese)
1 teaspoon vanilla extract
1/4 teaspoon ground cinnamon

Makes 2 cups
2 tablespoons contain approximately:
.5 gram of fiber
63 calories

Combine the date "sugar" and water in a saucepan and bring to a boil over medium heat. Reduce heat and simmer, uncovered, for about 20 minutes, or until all of the liquid is absorbed. Remove pan from the heat and cool to room temperature. When cool combine date mixture with all other ingredients and mix well in a blender. Store in the refrigerator. (Many people have told me it is hard to keep more than 1 or 2 days because someone in the family always finds it and eats it all up—right out of the container.)

This is my favorite dressing on fruit salad. It is also good served with a turkey dinner as an unusual replacement for cranberry sauce.

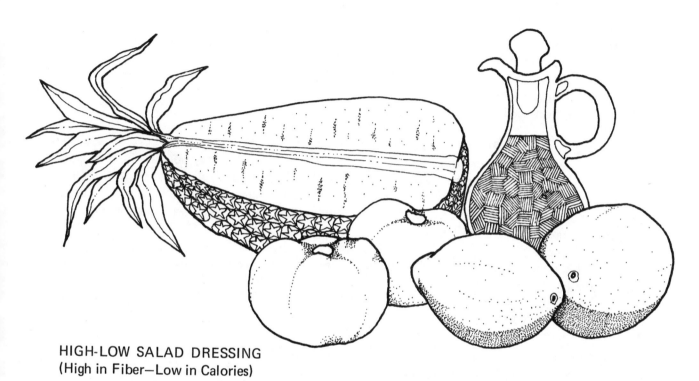

HIGH-LOW SALAD DRESSING
(High in Fiber—Low in Calories)

3/4 cup unsweetened pineapple juice
3/4 cup tomato juice
1 tablespoon fresh lemon juice
1/4 teaspoon salt
1 teaspoon date "sugar"
1 garlic bud, pressed
1/8 teaspoon freshly ground black pepper
1/8 teaspoon dry mustard

1 tablespoon chopped pimiento
1 teaspoon capers, chopped
1 tablespoon unprocessed wheat bran

Makes 1-1/2 cups
2 tablespoons contain approximately:
.2 gram of fiber
14 calories

Combine pineapple juice, tomato juice, lemon juice, salt and date "sugar." Mix thoroughly until salt is completely dissolved. Add all other ingredients and mix thoroughly. Store in a tightly covered container in the refrigerator. This is a divine salad dressing on all types of salad.

63

salads and salad dressings

SPINACH SALAD

1 tablespoon hulled sesame seeds
1 large red onion
2-1/2 pounds spinach, torn in bite-sized
    pieces (about 8 cups)
2 hard-cooked eggs, chopped
1/2 cup Lemon-Cheese Dressing, page 61

Makes 6 servings
Each serving contains approximately:
1.3 grams of fiber
115 calories

Preheat oven to 350°. Place the sesame seeds on a cookie sheet in the preheated oven for approximately 10 minutes or until a golden brown. Watch carefully as they burn easily. Set aside. Peel the onion and slice horizontally as thinly as possible. Separate each slice into rings. Combine the onion rings and all other ingredients, except the toasted sesame seeds, in a large mixing bowl and toss thoroughly. Serve the Spinach Salad on chilled plates and sprinkle each serving with 1/2 teaspoon of the toasted sesame seeds.

Variation I sometimes add more hard-cooked eggs or leftover chicken or meat to Spinach Salad and serve it as a luncheon entrée.

WATERCRESS SALAD

1/4 cup pine nuts
2 pounds watercress, torn in small pieces
    (about 6 cups)
1/2 cup finely chopped parsley
1/2 cup finely chopped chives
1/2 cup Lemon-Pepper Dressing, page 60

Makes 6 servings
Each serving contains approximately:
1.0 gram of fiber
139 calories

Preheat the oven to 350°. Place the pine nuts on a cookie sheet in the preheated oven for approximately 10 minutes or until golden brown. Watch carefully as they burn easily. Combine all ingredients in a large mixing bowl and toss thoroughly.
   Serve Watercress Salad on chilled plates with Pumpernickel Crisps or Cheese Straws. I particularly like this salad served with a barbecue dinner. It adds the perfect touch to the menu.

O'GREENERY SALAD

2 tablespoons sunflower seeds
2 large oranges, peeled and finely diced
1-1/2 pounds spinach, torn in bite-sized
   pieces (about 5 cups)
1 head Boston or butter lettuce, torn in
   bite-sized pieces (about 4 cups)

1/2 cup Mexican Fiber Dressing, page 60

Makes 6 servings
Each serving contains approximately:
1.5 grams of fiber
198 calories

Preheat the oven to 350°. Put the sunflower seeds on a cookie sheet in the preheated oven for approximately 10 minutes or until a golden brown. Watch carefully as they burn easily. Combine all ingredients in a large bowl and toss until every leaf glistens. Serve on chilled salad plates. The flavor of this salad is unusual and particularly good with plain broiled meat or poultry.

MARINATED MEXICAN SALAD

1 medium eggplant, finely diced
3 medium zucchini, finely diced
1 large tomato, finely diced
1/2 medium onion, finely chopped
1/2 cup Mexican Fiber Dressing, page 60
1/2 cup finely chopped parsley for garnish

Makes 8 servings
Each serving contains approximately:
.9 gram of fiber
128 calories

Cook the eggplant in a steamer until just fork tender, about 4 to 5 minutes. It is best to cook half of the diced eggplant at a time to avoid overcooking the bottom layer. Cook the diced zucchini in a steamer until just fork tender, about 4 to 5 minutes. Combine all ingredients in a 7- by 12-inch glass baking dish and mix thoroughly. Cover tightly and place in the refrigerator for at least 4 hours before serving. Sprinkle each serving with chopped parsley for garnish.

    I like to serve this salad on large lettuce leaves with a tablespoon of sour cream on the top. If you add 1 tablespoon of sour cream you will also be adding approximately 23 calories.

salads and salad dressings

GUACAMOLE SURPRISE

1 pound asparagus
1 tablespoon fresh lemon juice
1-1/2 tablespoons finely chopped onion
1 medium tomato, chopped
1 teaspoon salt
1/4 teaspoon ground cumin
1/4 teaspoon chili powder
1/8 teaspoon garlic powder
dash Tabasco sauce

1/2 cup sour cream
1 scant tablespoon (1 envelope) unflavored
   gelatin
1/4 cup water

Makes 2 cups
1/4 cup contains approximately:
.5 gram of fiber
47 calories

Wash the asparagus and break off the tough ends. Cut the spears into 1-inch pieces and cook in a steamer until just fork tender, about 4 minutes. Cool the cooked asparagus to room temperature. Put the cooled asparagus and all other ingredients, except the gelatin and water, into a blender and blend until smooth.

Put the gelatin in a small saucepan and add the water. Allow to soften for 5 minutes. Place the pan on low heat, stirring constantly, until the gelatin is completely dissolved. *Do not allow it to come to a boil.* Add the dissolved gelatin to the blender and blend on low speed until thoroughly mixed. Pour the guacamole in a bowl and refrigerate until firm.

Serve as a salad, dip, sauce or even a salad dressing. Surprise—no avocado!

SPORTSMAN SPECIAL
(An Overnight Salad)

2 cups tiny green peas (2 pounds
   unshelled)
1 medium head lettuce, torn in bite-sized
   pieces (about 4 cups)
1 medium onion, chopped
1/2 cup chopped green bell pepper
1/2 cup chopped celery
1-1/2 cups mayonnaise
2 tablespoons date "sugar"
4 teaspoons unprocessed wheat bran
1 cup grated sharp cheddar cheese

8 slices bacon, cooked crisp, well drained
   and crumbled (1/2 cup)
2 7-ounce cans water-pack chunk white
   tuna, drained
3 large tomatoes, cut in wedges, for garnish

Makes 8 servings
Each serving contains approximately:
1.6 grams of fiber
199 calories

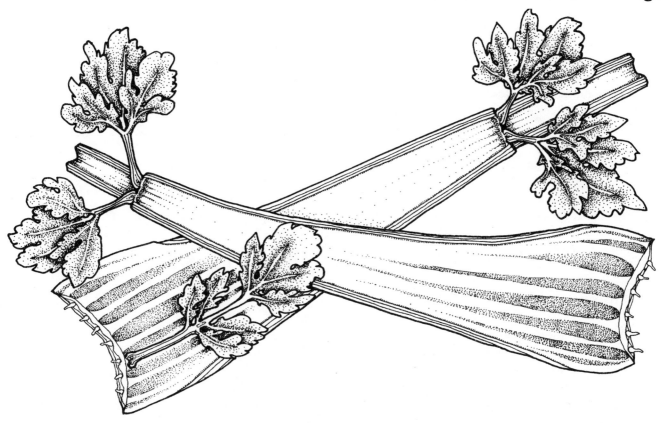

Wash the peas and dry thoroughly. Place them in a sealed plastic bag or a container with a tight-fitting lid and put them in the freezer until they are frozen hard, about 3 hours.

In a large salad bowl, place the ingredients in layers starting with the lettuce, then the onion, green pepper and celery. Separate the frozen peas if they are stuck together and evenly spread them over the celery layer. Combine the mayonnaise, date "sugar" and bran and mix well. Spoon it on top of the peas. Sprinkle the grated cheese evenly over the mayonnaise and then sprinkle the crumbled bacon on the cheese. *Do not stir.* Cover and refrigerate overnight.

Remove from the refrigerator, uncover, add drained tuna and toss well. Serve the salad on large cold plates, garnished with tomato wedges.

This is a "dream come true" luncheon dish for golfers and tennis players. You can invite the whole gang to come over for lunch directly from the golf course or tennis court and surprise them by serving a delicious luncheon salad in a matter of minutes. I like to serve toasted Wheat Berry Bread with this salad and Frozen Bonbons for dessert.

67

salads and salad dressings

CHEESE SALAD

1/4 cup sunflower seeds
3 cups julienne-cut Monterey Jack cheese
  (about 3/4 pound)
2 heads Boston or butter lettuce, torn in
  bite-sized pieces (about 8 cups)
2 cups thinly sliced mushrooms
2 cups alfalfa sprouts

1 cup mung bean sprouts
3/4 cup French Fiber Dressing, page 59

Makes 6 servings
Each serving contains approximately:
1.5 grams of fiber
397 calories

Preheat the oven to 350°. Put the sunflower seeds on a cookie sheet in the preheated oven for approximately 10 minutes or until a golden brown. Watch carefully as they burn easily. Combine all ingredients and toss until every leaf glistens. Serve on chilled plates. I like to serve Cheese Salad for a light supper with Onion Soup and toasted Wheat Berry Bread.

CRUDITÉ

2 medium potatoes, scrubbed and cut in julienne
2 large carrots, scrubbed and grated
2 medium beets, scrubbed and grated
2 medium turnips, scrubbed and grated
4 radishes, scrubbed and grated
1/2 onion, finely chopped
1/4 cup French Fiber Dressing, page 59

6 large red cabbage leaves
6 parsley sprigs

Makes 6 servings
Each serving contains approximately:
1.4 grams of fiber
140 calories

Steam the potatoes until just fork tender, cool and refrigerate until cold. Combine the carrots, beets, turnips, radishes and onion in a large mixing bowl. Add the potatoes and the dressing and mix well. Spoon each serving of this colorful salad onto a cabbage leaf and garnish it with a sprig of parsley for a delicious and beautiful salad or cold vegetable course.

This is the famous French salad made entirely of root vegetables. It was at one time considered beneath the dignity of the aristocracy to eat anything which grew beneath ground level and therefore these root vegetables were referred to as crude vegetables. Now we know they are high in vitamins, minerals and fiber but still the name of this root-vegetable salad remains. It is very good served before Sherried Chicken and Mushrooms on Rice.

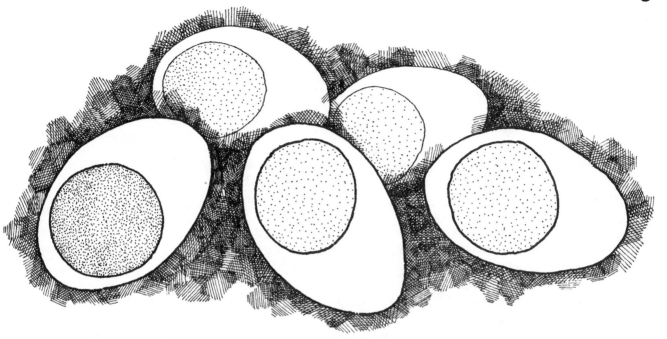

Variation Add 2 cups grated Monterey Jack cheese, 4 hard-cooked eggs, chopped, 2 cups shredded red cabbage and 1/4 cup more French Fiber Dressing for a delightfully different luncheon or light supper salad.

CRAB IN PAPAYA CUPS

2 ripe papayas
2 cups flaked cooked crab meat
2 tablespoons finely chopped chives or
    green onion tops
1/2 teaspoon curry powder
2 tablespoons sunflower seeds

parsley sprigs for garnish

Makes 4 servings
Each serving contains approximately:
1.8 grams of fiber
390 calories

Cut the papayas in half lengthwise and carefully remove all the seeds. Using a melon baller remove the papaya pulp from the peel, being careful not to tear the peeling. Combine the papaya balls and all other ingredients, except parsley sprigs, in a mixing bowl and mix well. Divide the mixture equally into the 4 papaya halves. Garnish each papaya cup with a sprig of fresh parsley.

    I love to serve this salad for a summer luncheon with warm Banana Muffins and iced tea.   69

salads and salad dressings

TWO-DAY LENTIL SALAD

2 cups lentils
1 orange, unpeeled and quartered
1 onion, halved
3 garlic buds, halved
2 bay leaves
1/8 teaspoon ground cloves
1 tablespoon salt
1 medium red onion, thinly sliced

2 tablespoons capers
1/2 cup Italian Fiber Dressing, page 59
1/2 cup finely chopped parsley

Makes 12 servings (7 cups)
Each serving contains approximately:
1.5 grams of fiber
154 calories

Soak lentils overnight in enough water to completely cover them. Drain the lentils and place in a large saucepan with enough fresh water to cover by 2 inches. Add the orange, halved onion, garlic, bay leaves, cloves and salt and mix well. Bring to a boil, reduce heat and simmer, covered, until lentils are tender but still firm, about 20 minutes.

Drain them immediately and discard orange, onion, garlic and bay leaves. Allow the lentils to cool to room temperature. Toss the cooled lentils with the sliced red onion, capers and salad dressing. Refrigerate all day or overnight before serving. Add the chopped parsley, mix thoroughly and serve on chilled plates.

This salad is marvelous for picnics or barbecue menus. I titled this recipe Two-Day Lentil Salad to alert you: You must start making it 2 days before you plan to serve it.

LEFTOVER LOUIS

1-1/2 heads lettuce, torn in bite-sized pieces
   (about 6 cups)
3 cups cold cooked fish or shellfish
2 hard-cooked eggs, sliced
2 large tomatoes, sliced
1-1/2 cups 1000 Island Dressing, page 57
6 asparagus spears, cooked and chilled

6 parsley sprigs for garnish (optional)

Makes 6 servings
Each serving contains approximately:
1.8 grams of fiber
270 calories

Arrange the lettuce on 6 large chilled plates. Place 1/2 cup of the cold fish or seafood on top of each serving. Garnish each salad with slices of hard-cooked egg and tomato. Spoon 1000 Island Dressing evenly over the top of each Louis. Place 1 asparagus spear on the top of each serving and garnish with a sprig of parsley.

I call this recipe Leftover Louis because I always plan to cook enough fish or shellfish to have some left over for a salad the next day. Of course you can use this recipe as an "original" and buy shrimp, crab, lobster or whatever you like best in a seafood Louis. However, many friends of mine never realized what a good Louis can be made from cold fish instead of shellfish until they had one at my house. Cold fish Louis is also much less expensive.

SALADE NUTTY NIÇOISE

1/2 cup chopped walnuts
1-1/2 heads lettuce, torn in bite-sized pieces
   (about 6 cups)
2 cups flaked tuna fish
1 cup diced cooked potatoes
2 cups cold cooked French-cut green beans
3/4 cup French Fiber Dressing, page 59
2 large tomatoes, quartered

4 teaspoons capers
4 anchovy fillets
2 pitted black olives, halved

Makes 4 servings
Each serving contains approximately:
2.4 grams of fiber
401 calories

Preheat the oven to 350°. Place the walnuts on a cookie sheet in the preheated oven for approximately 10 minutes or until a golden brown. Watch carefully as they burn easily. Set aside.

Divide lettuce in 4 chilled salad bowls. Put 1/2 cup tuna fish on top of the lettuce in each bowl. Combine the diced potatoes, green beans and salad dressing in another bowl and mix well. Spoon the mixture equally over each salad. Place 2 tomato quarters on each salad. Sprinkle 1 teaspoon of capers over salads. Decorate the top of each salad with an anchovy fillet topped with a black olive half. Sprinkle the toasted walnuts over the top of each salad.

Salade Niçoise is a classic French salad and is served throughout Europe. Like a French cassoulet it often varies from the "classic" ingredients and contains a variety of leftovers from the preceding day. This recipe can be varied according to the cold cooked vegetables you have in your refrigerator. I have already taken the liberty of adding nuts to this "classic" recipe which I think improves the taste *and* also adds fiber!

I serve Salade Nutty Niçoise with hot Roughage Rolls and Desert Lemon Chiffon Pie.

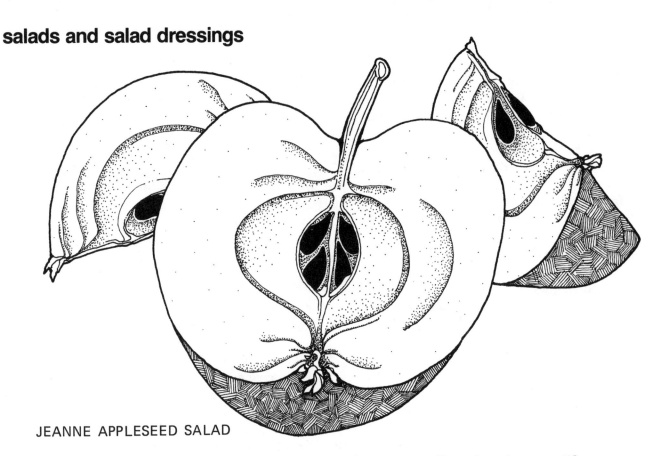

JEANNE APPLESEED SALAD

6 tablespoons sunflower seeds
2 medium heads iceberg lettuce, finely
   chopped (about 8 cups)
3 medium Delicious apples, diced
   (about 4 cups)
3 cups diced farmer cheese

3/4 cup Italian Fiber Dressing, page 59

Makes 6 servings
Each serving contains approximately:
2.0 grams of fiber
369 calories

Preheat the oven to 350°. Place the sunflower seeds on a cookie sheet in the preheated oven for approximately 10 minutes or until a golden brown. Watch carefully as they burn easily. Set aside. Combine all other ingredients and toss well. Serve on cold plates. Sprinkle 1 tablespoon of toasted sunflower seeds evenly over each serving.

    This is my own favorite salad. In fact, when I am at home working in my own kitchen it is also my usual lunch. I like it with toasted Wheat Berry Bread and plain yogurt sprinkled with date "sugar" for dessert.

COACHELLA VALLEY SALAD

3 tablespoons chopped almonds
1 cup (1/2 pint) low-fat cottage cheese
1/4 cup mayonnaise
2 tablespoons date "sugar"
1/4 teaspoon salt
2/3 cup grated carrots
2/3 cup finely shredded lettuce
1/3 cup sliced dates
4 crisp lettuce leaves

1 orange, peeled and sectioned
1 grapefruit, peeled and sectioned
4 carrot curls

Makes 4 servings
Each serving contains approximately:
1.7 grams of fiber
378 calories

Preheat oven to 350°. Put the chopped almonds on a cookie sheet in the preheated oven for approximately 10 minutes or until a golden brown. Watch carefully as they burn easily. Set aside.

Combine cottage cheese, mayonnaise, date "sugar" and salt and mix well. Add grated carrots, shredded lettuce, sliced dates and toasted almonds. Toss lightly until well mixed. Arrange lettuce leaves on 4 large chilled plates. Spoon salad mixture in center of leaves. Arrange orange and grapefruit sections around the salad. Place a carrot curl on the top of each salad.

This salad was created by Hilma Lawrence many years ago for the Sans Souci restaurant in Indio. She gave the recipe to my friends Gertrude and Hillman Yowell and they gave it to me. It is a deliciously different fruit salad and it looks just as beautiful as it tastes. I often serve it for luncheons with Banana Muffins, and I am grateful to Hilma and the Yowells each time I do!

HAWAIIAN COLE SLAW

1 head cabbage, finely shredded
1 cup (1/2 pint) sour cream
1/4 cup unprocessed wheat bran
1 cup crushed, fresh pineapple or canned in
    natural juice
1 tablespoon cider vinegar

1 tablespoon date "sugar"

Makes 8 servings
Each serving contains approximately:
1.0 gram of fiber
96 calories

Put the shredded cabbage in a colander and run cold water over it to wash it; dry thoroughly. Combine all other ingredients in a large bowl and mix thoroughly. Add the washed, thoroughly dried cabbage to the mixture in the bowl and mix it thoroughly again. This is the easiest, fastest and best-tasting cole slaw imaginable.

salads and salad dressings

FATIMA'S FIG SALAD

1/2 cup slivered almonds
1 cup thinly sliced dried figs (about 10 figs)
3 cups shredded cabbage
2 cups grated carrots
2 cups diced apples
1/2 cup Italian Fiber Dressing, page 59

Makes 6 servings
Each serving contains approximately:
3.5 grams of fiber
262 calories

Preheat the oven to 350°. Place the slivered almonds on a cookie sheet in the preheated oven for approximately 10 minutes or until a golden brown. Watch carefully as they burn easily. Combine all ingredients in a large bowl and mix thoroughly. Serve on very cold plates. I like to serve this salad with Company Lamb Chops.

POLYNESIAN PARTY SALAD

1 head lettuce, shredded (about 6 cups)
3 cups diced cooked turkey or chicken
2 cups diced pineapple
1 banana, thinly sliced
1/2 cup Fruit Salad Dressing, page 62
6 large lettuce leaves for garnish (optional)

12 macadamia nuts, finely chopped

Makes 6 servings
Each serving contains approximately:
1.2 grams of fiber
455 calories

Combine shredded lettuce with all other ingredients, except lettuce leaves you are going to use for garnish and macadamia nuts, and toss thoroughly. Place a lettuce leaf on each of 6 chilled plates. Divide the salad evenly on the 6 lettuce leaves. Sprinkle the chopped macadamia nuts evenly over the top of each serving. I like this salad for a luncheon entrée served with Curried Corn Muffins.

JEREMIAH'S WINTER FRUIT SALAD

1/2 cup chopped walnuts
1 head lettuce, finely chopped
1 medium onion, finely chopped
2 pears, diced
1/2 cup Green Goddess Dressing, page 55

Makes 8 servings
Each serving contains approximately:
1.6 grams of fiber
113 calories

74

Preheat the oven to 350°. Place the chopped walnuts on a cookie sheet in the preheated oven for approximately 10 minutes or until a golden brown. Watch carefully as they burn easily. Set aside. Combine all other ingredients in a large mixing bowl and mix well. Serve on chilled salad plates and sprinkle 1 tablespoon of toasted walnuts over each salad.

This is a particularly fun salad to serve when most fruits are out of season or unavailable. Jeremiah Goodman, the talented artist who illustrated my book, *Diet for a Happy Heart,* created this salad one winter afternoon when he wanted a fresh fruit salad and found the variety of fruit available was very limited. He then made it for me and I liked it so much I decided to include it here, with only slight variation.

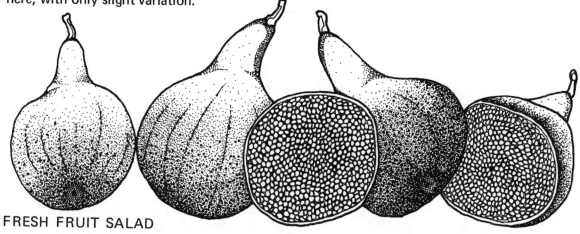

FRESH FRUIT SALAD

1/3 cup chopped walnuts
2 bananas, thinly sliced
2 red apples, diced
2 cups chopped celery
3/4 cup Date-Cheese Dressing, page 62
8 lettuce leaves

8 thin unpeeled orange slices for garnish (optional)

Makes 8 servings
Each serving contains approximately:
1.4 grams of fiber
130 calories

Preheat the oven to 350°. Place the walnuts on a cookie sheet in the preheated oven for approximately 10 minutes or until a golden brown. Watch carefully as they burn easily. Combine all ingredients, except the lettuce leaves and orange slices, in a large mixing bowl and mix well. Serve on lettuce leaves on chilled plates. Make a cut in each orange slice from the peel to the center. Twist each corner in opposite directions and place on top of salad for garnish.

vegetables

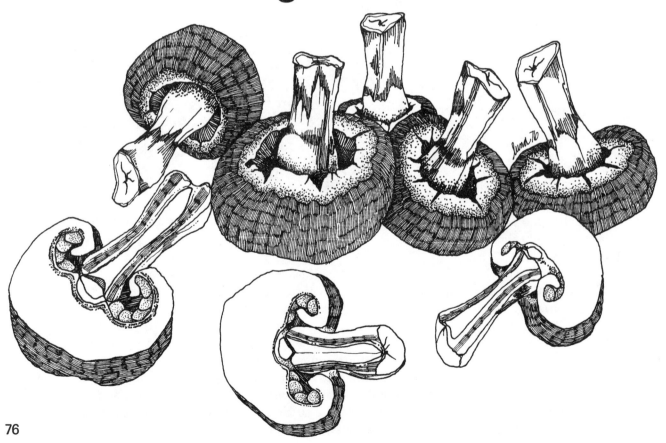

Vegetarians are no longer thought of as either members of a religious cult or a group of "food faddists." The number of vegetarians is rapidly rising and for the right reasons. The vegetarian diet, when properly balanced to include necessary amounts of protein and essential amino acids, offers not only enough available protein for body cell building but it is a far less expensive protein source than meat, higher in fiber and lower in both saturated and total fats. Plants are also better sources of many essential vitamins and minerals.

Vegetables are beautiful. When you are cooking them, keep them beautiful. Never overcook them to the point that they are limp and colorless.

Wash vegetables thoroughly. Then steam them, covered in very little water or cooking liquid, until they are "just done" or "crisp tender." If you are cooking green vegetables, either serve them immediately after cooking them or run them under cold water while they are still crisp; then reheat them to desired temperature just before serving. This will keep them a beautiful bright green color.

Don't try to preserve the green color by adding baking soda to the steaming water. The soda will also destroy most of the B vitamins and, in my opinion, it also adds a strange, unpleasant taste to the vegetables.

GLAZED ONIONS

2-1/2 pounds onions (4 large onions)
1 tablespoon corn oil
2 tablespoons unprocessed wheat bran

Makes about 2 cups
1/2 cup contains approximately:
1.8 grams of fiber
126 calories

The number of onions you use for this recipe depends upon the amount of Glazed Onions you need. I use at least 4 large onions because even if I am not using all of them, I can put the remainder in the refrigerator and reheat them to use as a garnish on steaks, chops, meat patties or even chicken.

Peel and slice onions very thinly. Pour the corn oil into a cured heavy iron skillet. Using a paper towel, wipe corn oil over entire inner surface of the skillet. Heat the skillet over medium heat and add the thinly sliced onions and bran. Cook over medium heat, stirring frequently, for 30 minutes. Continue cooking the onions and bran, stirring occasionally, over low heat for another 30 minutes or a little longer if necessary to lightly brown the onions.

I serve Glazed Onions on Nut Burgers or ground meat burgers. They are also delicious served on sautéed liver.

vegetables

DILLED ONIONS LAUTREC

2-2/3 cups white distilled vinegar
3-1/2 tablespoons salt
1-3/4 cups date "sugar"
4 teaspoons dillweed
1-1/3 cups water
5 large white onions, very thinly sliced

Makes 2 quarts
Each 1/2 cup contains approximately:
1.0 gram of fiber
90 calories

Combine vinegar and salt and stir until salt is dissolved. Add date "sugar," dillweed and water and mix well. Put the onions in a large non-metal container with a lid and pour the liquid mixture over them. Stir the onions around in the liquid. Cover and refrigerate for at least 24 hours before serving.

Dilled Onions Lautrec will keep for weeks in the refrigerator and the flavor will continue to improve. I serve them with many cold meat, fish and poultry dishes. They are also good in salads.

I was given this recipe by Dorothy Sorensen, the charming owner of a delightful little French sidewalk cafe in La Jolla, California. I have varied her recipe just a bit to increase the fiber, but the flavor remains the same.

BRAN-BAKED RHUBARB

1 pound rhubarb, cut in 1-inch pieces
   (about 4 cups)
2 teaspoons grated orange peel
1/2 cup date "sugar"
1/4 cup unprocessed wheat bran
3 tablespoons fresh orange juice

1 tablespoon butter or corn oil margarine

Makes 2-1/2 cups
1/2 cup contains approximately:
1.9 grams of fiber
130 calories

Preheat oven to 350°. Combine all ingredients except butter or margarine, mix well and put in a greased 1-1/2-quart casserole with a lid. Dot evenly with the butter or margarine. Cover and bake in the preheated oven for 40 minutes. This is a nice change for a vegetable dish and is particularly good served with pork or ham.

BRUSSELS SPROUTS IN HERB BUTTER

1 pound Brussels sprouts
3 tablespoons butter or corn oil margarine
1/4 teaspoon salt
1 teaspoon sweet basil
1/4 cup minced parsley
1/4 cup minced chives or green onion tops

2 teaspoons unprocessed wheat bran

Makes 8 servings
Each serving contains approximately:
1.0 gram of fiber
78 calories

Steam Brussels sprouts until just crisp tender, about 10 to 12 minutes. Melt butter or margarine, add all other ingredients and cook for 5 minutes over low heat. Add the cooked Brussels sprouts to the herb-butter sauce and mix thoroughly.

If you are making this dish ahead of time, run cold water over the cooked Brussels sprouts to keep them green and then reheat them in the butter sauce.

Variations Many other green vegetables are delicious prepared in this manner. I have used Brussels sprouts as my example because many people who do not particularly care for this vegetable love them prepared this way. If you *really* don't like Brussels sprouts, try this recipe with broccoli, asparagus, or thinly sliced zuchinni instead.

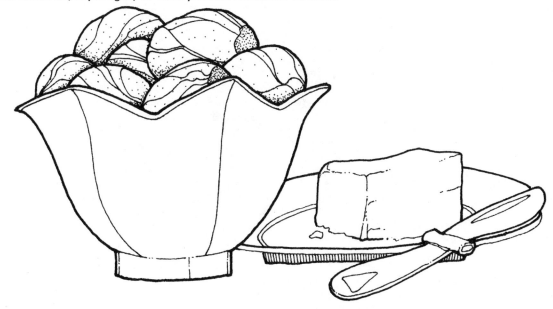

vegetables

ARTICHOKE APPETIZERS

12 tiny artichokes (or 6 large artichokes)
2 garlic buds, peeled and halved
1 slice lemon
water
1-1/2 cups Creamy Curry Dressing, page 58

Makes 6 servings
Each serving contains approximately:
5.1 grams of fiber
401 calories

Wash artichokes well and pull off tough outer leaves. Holding each artichoke by its stem, cut the tips off the leaves with scissors. When trimming the tips, start at the bottom of the artichoke and work your way to the top in a spiral pattern. Trim off the stem, turn artichoke upside down and press firmly to open it up as much as possible.

Pour water to a depth of 2 inches in the bottom of a saucepan. Add garlic, lemon slice and salt, then bring to a boil. Place artichokes in boiling water, cover tightly and cook over medium heat about 25 minutes for small artichokes or 40 minutes for large artichokes, or until stems can be easily pierced with a fork.

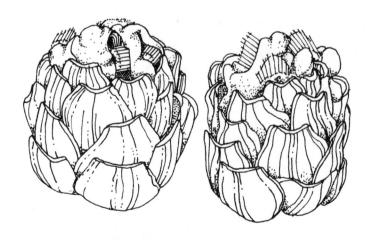

Remove artichokes from water and place upside down to drain until cool enough to handle easily. Remove the center leaves and spread the artichoke open very carefully. Reach down into the center and remove the furry choke, pulling it out a little at a time. Be sure to remove the entire choke so you will have a clean, edible artichoke bowl.

When serving large artichokes place each on an artichoke plate, if you have them, or a dinner plate, and serve the Creamy Curry Dressing on the side to use as a dip for the leaves.

When serving the tiny artichokes spoon the Creamy Curry Dressing into the center of each artichoke and serve 2 per person on chilled salad plates. Or you can pass them as hors d'oeuvre, if they are small enough and only the innermost leaves are left so that the entire tiny artichoke heart is edible.

Variations One of my favorite first courses is to use the large "artichoke bowls" as a first course filled with a cold, jelled soup—you can literally serve the soup in the salad! "Artichoke bowls" are also an excellent and beautiful cold luncheon entrée filled with a chicken or seafood salad. Serve the artichoke bowl hot, filled with either rice or another-colored vegetable such as carrots or beets for an unusual hot vegetable side dish. You can also fill the hot artichokes with hot fish, chicken or meat filling.

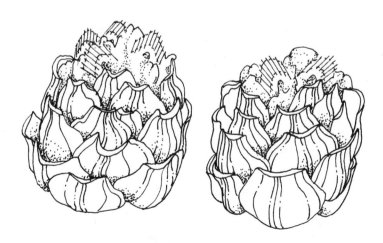

vegetables

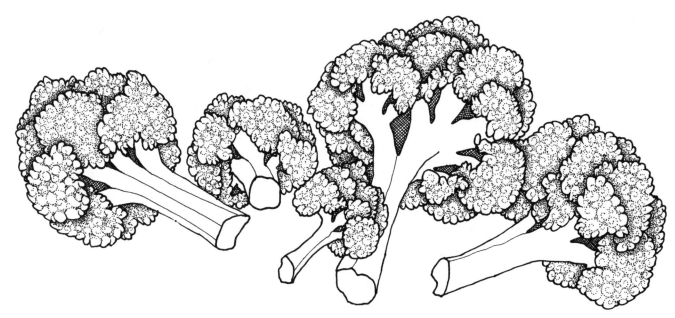

CURRIED CAULIFLOWER
(Side Dish, Dip or Sauce)

1 large head cauliflower
1 medium onion, finely chopped
3/4 teaspoon salt
1/8 teaspoon white pepper
1/2 cup water
1 cup low-fat milk
2 teaspoons butter or corn oil margarine
1 tablespoon whole wheat flour
1/4 cup unprocessed wheat bran

1 teaspoon curry powder
1/4 teaspoon ground ginger
1/4 teaspoon Worcestershire sauce
1 teaspoon fresh lemon juice

Makes about 4 cups
1/2 cup contains approximately:
1.0 gram of fiber
58 calories

Break cauliflower into flowerets and place in a large saucepan with a lid. Add the onion, salt and pepper. Add the water and bring to a boil. Reduce heat and simmer until fork tender, about 15 to 20 minutes. Put the cooked cauliflower mixture and its cooking liquid in the blender and blend until a smooth creamy texture.

While the cauliflower is cooking, put the milk in a saucepan and place over low heat. In another saucepan, melt the butter or margarine and add the flour, stirring constantly. Cook the flour and butter mixture for 3 minutes. Do not brown. Take the flour-butter mixture off the heat and add the simmering milk all at once, stirring constantly with a wire whisk. Put the sauce back on low heat and cook for 20 minutes, stirring occasionally. Remove from the heat and add all remaining ingredients including the puréed cauliflower-onion mixture. Return to low heat and heat just to serving temperature.

This is an unusual vegetable side dish. I particularly like it served with broiled chicken or fish. Or chill it for a low calorie dip. Your friends will never guess what it is! The sauce is also excellent on other vegetables such as fresh green peas or beans.

MILANESE STUFFED MUSHROOMS

12 very large or 18 medium mushrooms
1/4 cup chicken stock
1-1/2 cups low-fat milk
1 tablespoon butter or corn oil margarine
1-1/2 tablespoons whole wheat flour
1/2 teaspoon salt
1/8 teaspoon white pepper
1/8 teaspoon ground nutmeg
1/2 teaspoon oregano
1/4 teaspoon sweet basil

1/4 cup unprocessed wheat bran
1/2 cup grated Romano cheese
1/2 cup finely chopped tomato
1/4 cup chopped parsley

Makes 12 large or 18 medium mushrooms
Each large mushroom contains approximately:
.5 gram of fiber
54 calories

Wash mushrooms and remove stems; set the mushroom caps aside to use later. Chop the mushroom stems and put them in a saucepan with the chicken stock. Bring to a boil, reduce the heat, cover and simmer for 10 minutes.

While the mushroom stems are cooking, put the milk in a saucepan on low heat and bring to the boiling point. In another saucepan, melt the butter or margarine and add the flour, stirring constantly. Cook the flour and butter for 3 minutes; do not brown. Remove the flour mixture from the heat and add the simmering milk all at once, stirring constantly with a wire whisk. Put the sauce back on low heat and cook 30 minutes, stirring occasionally. Preheat the oven to 350°.

Put the cooked mushroom stems and their cooking liquid into a blender and blend until smooth. Add the puréed mushroom stems to the sauce. Add all remaining ingredients except the mushroom caps and mix well. Put the mushroom caps into a greased baking dish and fill each mushroom with sauce, dividing it evenly. Bake, covered, in the preheated oven 40 minutes.

vegetables

MINTED PEAS

4 cups green peas (4 pounds unshelled)
2 teaspoons arrowroot
1/2 cup water
2 teaspoons date "sugar"
2 tablespoons butter or corn oil margarine
1/2 teaspoon salt

1/2 cup minced fresh mint leaves

Makes 8 servings
Each serving contains approximately:
1.5 grams of fiber
96 calories

Steam peas until they are crisp tender, about 2 minutes. Be careful not to overcook them. Dissolve arrowroot in water, add the date "sugar" and cook, stirring constantly, over medium heat until mixture comes to a boil. Stir until it is clear and thickened, about 2 minutes. Remove from heat and add the butter or margarine and salt. Pour over the steamed peas. Add fresh mint and toss, mixing all ingredients thoroughly.

Variation This recipe is also delicious made with carrots.

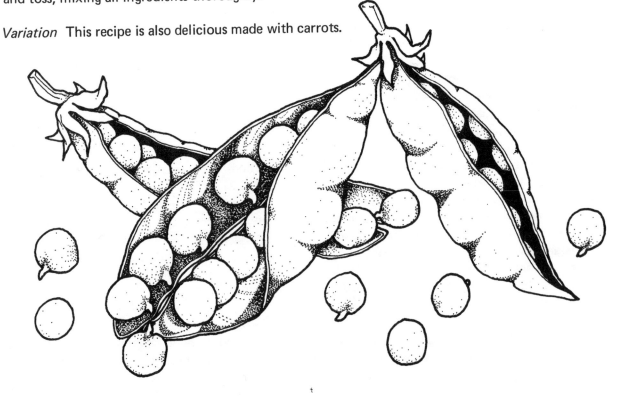

FLUFFY BROWN RICE

1 cup long-grain brown rice
2 cups water
2 cups chicken stock
1/2 teaspoon salt (or to taste; depends on
   saltiness of chicken stock)

Makes 3 cups
1/2 cup contains approximately:
.3 gram of fiber
89 calories

Combine the rice and water and allow to stand for 1 hour. Drain rice thoroughly and set aside. Pour the chicken stock and salt into a 2-quart saucepan with a lid. Bring the chicken stock to a boil and add the rice. Bring back to a boil and then turn the heat to low. Cover and cook for 50 minutes. Turn the heat off, but do not remove the pan from the burner. Remove the lid and allow the rice to stand for 10 minutes before serving.

BROWN-BERRIED RICE

1 cup long-grain brown rice
1/2 cup wheat berries
2 cups water
2-1/2 cups chicken stock
1/2 teaspoon salt (or to taste; depends on
   saltiness of chicken stock)

Makes 4 cups
1/2 cup contains approximately:
.4 gram of fiber
114 calories

Combine rice, wheat berries and water. Allow to soak for 1 hour. Drain thoroughly and set aside. Pour the chicken stock and salt into a 2-quart saucepan with a lid. Bring the chicken stock to a boil and add the rice and wheat berries. Bring back to a boil and turn the heat to low. Cover and cook for 50 minutes. Turn the heat off, but do not remove the pan from the burner. Remove the lid and allow the Brown-Berried Rice to stand for 10 minutes before serving.

vegetables

WILD RICE and WALNUTS

3/4 cup wild rice (4 ounces)
1-1/2 cups chicken stock
1-1/2 teaspoons soy sauce
1/2 teaspoon thyme
1/2 cup chopped walnuts
1 tablespoon butter or corn oil margarine
1 medium onion, chopped

1 celery stalk , without leaves, chopped

Makes 3 cups
1/2 cup contains approximately:
.5 gram of fiber
134 calories

Combine the wild rice, chicken stock, soy sauce and thyme in a saucepan with a lid. Bring to a boil, reduce heat, cover and simmer for about 30 to 35 minutes or until all the liquid is absorbed and the rice is fluffy. Remove from the heat and set aside.

Preheat the oven to 350°. While the rice is cooking, toast the walnuts in the preheated oven for about 10 to 15 minutes. Watch them carefully as they burn easily.

Melt the butter or margarine and add the chopped onion and celery. Cook over medium heat until the onion is clear and tender. Combine the cooked rice, toasted walnuts, cooked onion and celery and mix well.

I served Wild Rice and Walnuts last Christmas with turkey instead of more traditional bread dressing and received raves from all my guests.

CHRISTMAS RICE
(It's Red and Green)

1 cup long grain brown rice
2 cups water
2 tablespoons butter or corn oil margarine
1 cup finely chopped onion
2 cups tomato sauce
1 cup chicken stock
1/2 cup dry red wine
1 teaspoon salt
1/4 teaspoon freshly ground black pepper

1/2 cup diced tomato
2 cups French-cut green beans
1/4 cup grated Romano or Parmesan cheese

Makes 4 cups
1/2 cup contains approximately:
1.3 grams of fiber
245 calories

Combine rice and water and soak for 1 hour. Drain rice and set aside. In a large, heavy iron skillet, melt the butter or margarine. Add the rice and chopped onion. Cook for about 10 minutes, stirring occasionally. Add the tomato sauce, chicken stock, wine, salt and pepper. Mix well. Cover and simmer for about 1-1/2 hours or until the rice is tender and all liquid is absorbed. Stir in chopped tomato and green beans and sprinkle the grated cheese on the top. Cover and heat thoroughly.

CRUNCHY CRACKED WHEAT

2 cups chicken stock
1/2 teaspoon salt (or to taste; depends on saltiness of chicken stock)
1 cup cracked wheat (bulgur)

Makes 3 cups
1/2 cup contains approximately:
.7 gram of fiber
80 calories

Bring chicken stock and salt to a boil. Add the cracked wheat and bring back to a boil. Cover and reduce heat to low. Cook 20 minutes and turn heat off but leave the pan on the burner. Remove lid and allow to stand for 10 minutes before serving.

SOYBEAN SNACKS

2 cups soybeans
4 cups water
cottonseed oil for deep frying
salt

Makes 6 cups
1/4 cup contains approximately:
.8 gram of fiber
78 calories

Wash the soybeans and drain them. Remove any discolored beans. Put the washed soybeans in a container with a lid and pour the water over the beans. Cover and soak overnight. Drain the soybeans thoroughly and spread them out on towels to dry at room temperature.

Heat the oil in a deep fryer or deep frying pan to 250°, then add 1 cup soybeans and cook for approximately 20 minutes, or until lightly browned. Remove from the oil onto paper towels to blot or remove excess oil. Salt lightly. Cool completely before putting in bowls or jars. Store in a jar with a tight-fitting lid. If you want them crisper, place on cookie sheet in a 350° oven for about 10 minutes, or until they reach desired crispness.

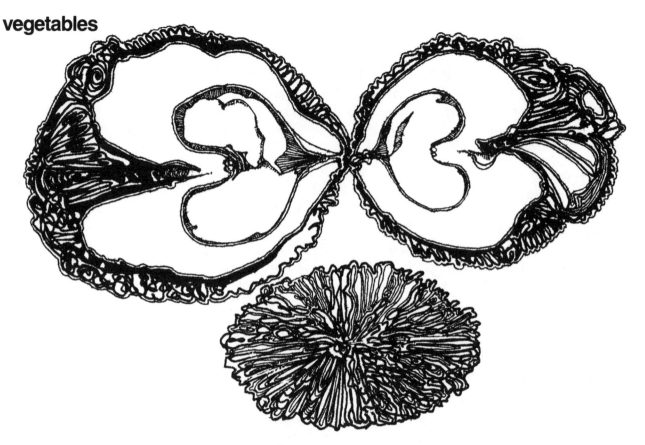

NUT BURGERS

3 tablespoons butter or corn oil margarine
1/4 cup finely chopped onion
1 cup whole wheat bread crumbs
1 cup cooked oatmeal
1 egg, slightly beaten
1 cup chopped walnuts
1-1/2 teaspoons soy sauce

1/2 teaspoon thyme
1/4 teaspoon sage

Makes 6 burgers
Each burger contains approximately:
.6 gram of fiber
257 calories

Heat the butter or margarine in a cured heavy iron skillet. Add the onion and cook until tender. Remove the onion and put it in a large mixing bowl. *Do not wash the skillet.*

Add all remaining ingredients to the onion and mix well. Form into 6 patties and cook in the same skillet used for the onion until a golden brown on both sides.

VEGETABLE MEDLEY AU GRATIN

1 tablespoon corn oil
1 medium onion, minced
2 garlic buds, minced
1/2 teaspoon thyme
1 bay leaf
6 medium tomatoes, peeled and diced
1 teaspoon salt
1 teaspoon oregano
1 teaspoon freshly ground black pepper
1 small eggplant, diced
4 medium zucchini, diced
1/2 green bell pepper, seeded and diced
1/4 cup unprocessed wheat bran
1/4 cup grated Romano cheese

1/4 teaspoon ground nutmeg
2 cups finely chopped spinach
 (about 1/2 pound)
1 cup minced parsley
1/4 cup chopped chives
1 tablespoon sweet basil
1 cup grated Monterey Jack cheese
paprika

Makes 6 servings
Each serving contains approximately:
3.1 grams of fiber
191 calories

Preheat the oven to 350°. Heat the corn oil in a pan with a lid. Add the onion, garlic, thyme and bay leaf. Cover and cook for 5 minutes. Add the diced tomatoes, salt, oregano and pepper and mix well. Cover and cook for 10 more minutes.

While the sauce is cooking put the diced eggplant in a steamer. Cover and cook for 5 minutes. Add the steamed eggplant, zucchini and bell pepper to the tomato sauce and cook, covered, for about 12 to 15 minutes. Remove the vegetables from the heat and add the bran, Romano cheese, nutmeg, spinach, parsley, chives and sweet basil and mix well.

Divide the vegetable mixture equally into 6 au gratin dishes or individual baking dishes. Sprinkle one-sixth of the grated Jack cheese over each serving. Sprinkle a little paprika over the top of each dish for color. (If you do not have individual dishes put all the vegetables into one large casserole and sprinkle all the cheese over the top. Then after baking, divide into 6 servings.) Bake, uncovered, in the preheated oven for 15 minutes.

This is very similar to a vegetable and cheese casserole served at The Golden Door, the world famous health spa in Escondido, California. Their talented chef, Michel Stoot, taught us how to bake this popular Golden Door entrée at his weekly cooking class during my own week at The Golden Door last fall. I have changed his recipe slightly to increase the fiber content, but the calories remain the same.

vegetables

ZUCCHINI ZINGER
(For people who think they don't like zucchini.)

4 cups thinly sliced zucchini (about 1 pound)
2 cups (1 pound) ricotta cheese
1/4 cup unprocessed wheat bran
1/2 cup finely chopped onion
1/4 cup finely chopped parsley
1-1/2 teaspoons oregano
1/4 teaspoon salt
1 cup tomato sauce

3/4 cup grated mozzarella cheese
1/4 cup grated Parmesan cheese

Makes 6 servings
Each serving contains approximately:
1.1 grams of fiber
189 calories

Preheat oven to 350°. Cook the zucchini in a steamer until just fork tender, about 2 to 3 minutes. Drain the zucchini and set aside. Combine the ricotta cheese, bran, onion, parsley, oregano, salt and tomato sauce and mix. Add the cooked zucchini and again mix well. Pour the mixture into a baking dish or casserole and sprinkle the mozzarella cheese over the top. Then sprinkle the Parmesan cheese evenly over the top of the mozzarella cheese. Bake, uncovered, in the preheated oven for 20 minutes.

I like to serve Zucchini Zinger with sliced tomatoes and garlic bread.

FETTUCCINI FLORENTINE

4 cups cooked Fiber Fettuccini Pasta, page 152
4 cups Florentine Sauce, page 46

Makes 6 servings
Each serving contains approximately:
2.3 grams of fiber
356 calories

Combine the cooked pasta with the Florentine Sauce and toss lightly until well mixed. Serve on large plates with broiled tomatoes.

This is one of my very favorite Italian dishes and is occasionally a welcome change from the tomato sauces usually served with pasta.

CHILI SIN CARNE

1-1/2 cups pinto beans
1/2 cup wheat berries
6 cups water
2 tablespoons corn oil
2 medium onions, chopped
2 garlic buds, finely chopped
1 tablespoon chili powder
1 teaspoon ground cumin
1/2 teaspoon oregano
2 teaspoons salt
1/8 teaspoon freshly ground black pepper

2 green jalapeño chilies, seeded and finely
  chopped
4 large tomatoes, diced
1-1/2 cups grated sharp cheddar cheese
3/4 cup finely chopped chives or green
  onion tops

Makes 6 servings
Each serving contains approximately:
3.6 grams of fiber
396 calories

Put the beans and wheat berries in a large pot or Dutch oven, add the water and soak overnight. Next day bring them to a boil in the same water, reduce heat and simmer 2 hours or until tender.

Heat the oil in a large, cured heavy iron skillet. Add the onions and garlic and cook until tender. Add the chili powder, cumin, oregano, salt and pepper and mix well. Add the jalapeño chilies and tomatoes, mix well and simmer for 30 minutes. Then add the seasoned vegetables to the beans and mix well. Serve in large bowls and garnish with grated cheese and chopped chives or green onion tops. I serve this chili with toasted tortillas and Guacamole Surprise.

vegetables

FRIJOLES REFRITOS CON QUESO
(Refried Beans with Cheese)

1 pound (2-1/4 cups) pinto beans
6 cups water
2 tablespoons corn oil
1 medium onion, minced
2 garlic buds, minced
1 tablespoon chili powder
2 teaspoons salt

1/2 cup tomato sauce
2 cups grated sharp cheddar cheese

Makes 8 servings
Each serving contains approximately:
2.7 grams of fiber
315 calories

Put the beans in a large pan or soup kettle. Add the water and soak all day or overnight. Bring the beans to a boil in the same water. Reduce the heat and simmer about 2 hours or until tender. *Do not drain the beans.* You will need the liquid in this recipe.

Heat the oil in a large, cured heavy iron skillet. Add the onion and garlic and cook until tender, about 5 minutes. Add the chili powder, salt and tomato sauce and mix well. Remove the beans from the liquid, reserving the liquid, and mash them. Add the mashed beans to the skillet, about a cup at a time, adding enough bean liquid each time to keep the bean mixture moist but not soupy.

Continue adding the beans and reserved bean liquid until you have added all of the beans. Stir 1 cup of the grated cheese into the beans. Sprinkle the remaining cup of cheese over the top and allow it to melt before serving.

Frijoles Refritos con Queso is a favorite all over Mexico and in many parts of the United States, where beans are served with almost every meal, including breakfast. This is my own favorite recipe for refried beans. It makes a good vegetable side dish or to use it for a great vegetarian meal, serve it with brown rice and fresh tomatoes. I also use this recipe to make Tostadas.

TOSTADAS

8 corn tortillas, toasted
salt
1 cup Frijoles Refritos con Queso, preceding
2 cups shredded sharp cheddar cheese
8 cups Gazpacho, page 35
2 heads lettuce, shredded (about 10 cups)
2 large ripe tomatoes, diced

1/2 cup Mexican Fiber Dressing, page 60
1/4 cup sour cream

Makes 8 servings
Each serving contains approximately:
2.4 grams of fiber
328 calories

Preheat the oven to 400°. Place the tortillas on a cookie sheet and salt lightly. Bake them in the preheated oven for 10 minutes. Remove from the oven and spread each tortilla with 2 tablespoons of the refried beans. Sprinkle 1/4 cup cheese on each tortilla. Put the tortillas back in the oven for 3 more minutes or until the cheese has melted. Remove from the oven and place each tortilla on a large plate. Pour 1/2 cup Gazpacho over each serving.

Toss the lettuce, tomatoes and dressing together well. Divide the salad evenly on top of the tortillas. Pour one more 1/2 cup Gazpacho over each evenly and spoon 1/2 tablespoon of sour cream on top of each serving.

Tostadas make a great Mexican luncheon dish. I usually serve Bran-Mango Mousse for dessert. Or if mangoes are not in season, I serve Bran-Baked Applesauce instead.

Variation Substitute Guacamole Surprise for the sour cream on the top. This is delicious and lowers the calories. If you wish to add a meat on the Tostada, I suggest 4 cups diced cooked chicken. This will increase the calories 140 per serving.

eggs and cheese

Neither eggs nor cheese contain any dietary fiber, but both combine well with high fiber foods, adding great variety and taste appeal to a high fiber diet. Many of my favorite vegetarian entrées are a combination of high fiber vegetables and cheese or eggs—or both.

Eggs should be very fresh. Old eggs have thin, watery whites which are not good for beating and don't even make pretty poached eggs.

The number of eggs per week should be limited by anyone on a low-cholesterol diet. If you are not sure about the number of eggs you should include in your diet, check with your doctor.

CURRIED EGGS

8 eggs, hard cooked
2 cups low-fat milk
4 teaspoons butter or corn oil margarine
2-1/2 tablespoons whole wheat pastry flour
1/8 teaspoon salt
dash white pepper
1/4 cup unprocessed wheat bran
1 teaspoon curry powder

1/2 teaspoon ground ginger
1/4 teaspoon Worcestershire sauce
1 teaspoon fresh lemon juice

Makes 8 servings
Each serving contains approximately:
.4 gram of fiber
144 calories

Preheat the oven to 350°. Cut the eggs in half lengthwise. Remove yolks, being careful not to tear the egg white. Arrange the egg whites in a 9-inch glass pie pan or shallow baking dish. Mash the egg yolks or rub them through a sieve; set aside.

Put the milk in a saucepan on low heat. In another saucepan melt the butter or margarine and add the whole wheat pastry flour, stirring constantly. Cook the flour and butter for 3 minutes. Do not brown. Take the flour-butter mixture off the heat and add the simmering milk all at once, stirring constantly with a wire whisk. Put the sauce back on low heat and cook slowly for 20 minutes, stirring occasionally. When the sauce is cooked, remove from heat, add all remaining ingredients and mix well.

Add 1/2 cup of sauce to the mashed egg yolk and mix well. Fill the 16 egg white halves equally with the egg yolk mixture. Pour remaining sauce over the tops of the eggs evenly.

Bake in the preheated oven for 20 minutes or until the eggs are lightly browned. This is a great "make ahead of time" brunch entrée dish. I serve it with Tropical Ham Slices and Orange Bread.

eggs and cheese

GREEN EGGS AND HAM EN CROUSTADE
(A Salute to Dr. Seuss!)

1 loaf whole wheat bread, unsliced
2 tablespoons butter or corn oil margarine,
   melted
8 eggs
1/2 cup low-fat milk
1/2 cup chopped parsley
1/4 cup chopped fresh chives or green
   onion tops
1/2 teaspoon tarragon
1/2 teaspoon salt

1/8 teaspoon white pepper
1 tablespoon butter or corn oil margarine
1 cup chopped, cooked ham
1 tablespoon finely chopped chives or
   green onion tops for garnish
6 parsley sprigs for garnish

Makes 4 servings
Each serving contains approximately:
.6 gram of fiber
399 calories

Preheat the oven to 325°. Slice the top crust off of the loaf of bread. Carefully hollow out the loaf leaving walls 3/4 inch thick. (I keep the bread crumbs in a sealed bag in the freezer to use in other recipes calling for whole wheat bread crumbs.) Using a pastry brush, evenly apply the melted butter or margarine to the entire croustade. Place it on a cookie sheet in the preheated oven for about 25 minutes or until it is well toasted. Remove to a serving platter and keep warm.

Put the eggs in a bowl and beat them until they are frothy. Put the milk, parsley, chives, tarragon, salt and white pepper in a blender and blend until smooth in texture. Pour the *green* mixture into the eggs and mix thoroughly.

Melt the butter or margarine in a large skillet and heat the skillet well before adding the eggs. Add the egg mixture and reduce heat, stirring the eggs constantly until they are almost set. Add the ham and cook until eggs are desired consistency. Be careful not to overcook the eggs as it makes them too dry.

Remove the eggs from the heat and spoon them into the croustade which has been placed on a serving platter. Sprinkle the chopped chives over the top of the eggs and decorate the platter with sprigs of parsley.

Theodor (Dr. Seuss) Geisel is one of my favorite authors. Ted and his charming wife, Audrey, are also two of my favorite people. She is both a fabulous cook and an outstanding hostess. Since the publication of his book *Green Eggs and Ham* in 1960 they have been served this dish more times and in more ways than they can remember (or want to)! This is the most elegant presentation of the "classic combination" I could dream up in their honor. I suggest serving it with sliced fresh fruit or Broiled Bananas.

SPINACH SOUFFLÉ

1 cup low-fat milk
2 tablespoons butter or corn oil margarine
3 tablespoons whole wheat pastry flour
3 egg yolks
1/2 teaspoon salt
1/2 teaspoon oregano
1/4 teaspoon white pepper
1/4 teaspoon ground nutmeg
1/3 cup grated Romano or Parmesan cheese
1 tablespoon unprocessed wheat bran

1/2 cup chopped, cooked and well drained
    spinach (about 1/2 pound raw)
5 egg whites, at room temperature
pinch salt
1/8 teaspoon cream of tartar

Makes 4 servings
Each serving contains approximately:
.6 gram of fiber
257 calories

Preheat oven to 400°. Put milk in a saucepan on low heat. Put butter or margarine in another, large saucepan. Melt butter and add flour, stirring constantly. Cook the flour and butter for 3 minutes. (This is so your flour will be cooked, thus avoiding a raw flour taste in your soufflé.) Take the flour-butter mixture off the heat and pour in the hot milk, which should be at the boiling point, all at once, rapidly stirring with a wire whisk. Put the pan back on the heat and allow to come to a boil, stirring constantly. Boil for 1 to 2 minutes. At this point the sauce will be quite thick. Remove from the heat. Add the 3 egg yolks one at a time, stirring in each one thoroughly with a wire whisk. Add the salt, oregano, white pepper and nutmeg. *Stop!*

You can make this much of the soufflé ahead of time if you are entertaining. Cover the saucepan, reheat the mixture to lukewarm before adding the other ingredients and the beaten egg whites. Or you can go right ahead and finish the soufflé; it will be ready in 25 to 30 minutes. Add the cheese, bran and cooked spinach to the sauce and stir well. Put the egg whites in a large mixing bowl. Add a pinch of salt and the cream of tartar. Beat whites until stiff. Add one-fourth of the egg whites to the cheese-spinach sauce and stir them in. This lightens the sauce. Add the remaining egg whites to the sauce and very carefully fold them in, being sure not to overmix. Pour the mixture into an 8-inch greased and floured soufflé dish. Place it in the center of the preheated 400° oven. Immediately turn the oven down to 375°. Cook the soufflé 25 to 30 minutes and serve immediately. There is an old saying, "You can wait for a soufflé but a soufflé cannot wait for you!"

Spinach Soufflé is a lovely entrée either for lunch or light supper. I like to serve it with sliced tomatoes and Pumpernickel Crisps. It also makes an unusual vegetable side dish.

eggs and cheese

KAKI'S SPOOF SOUFFLÉ

1 tablespoon corn oil
1/2 medium onion, finely chopped
1 small (or 1/2 large) eggplant, peeled and
   diced (3 cups)
1 small zucchini, thinly sliced (1 cup)
1/2 cup grated sharp cheddar cheese
1 cup grated mozzarella cheese
2 eggs, beaten frothy
1/2 teaspoon salt

1/4 teaspoon sweet basil
1/8 teaspoon white pepper
1/2 teaspoon oregano
2 tablespoons unprocessed wheat bran

Makes 4 servings as an entrée
Each serving contains approximately:
2.2 grams of fiber
244 calories

Preheat the oven to 350°. Heat oil over medium heat in a large pan with a lid. Add the onion and cook, covered, for 5 minutes. Add the eggplant to the onion and cook, covered, for 10 more minutes, being careful not to burn. Remove the pan from the heat. Add the zucchini to the onion and eggplant mixture and mix well.

Put one-half of the mixture in a greased 1-1/2-quart casserole. Combine the cheddar cheese and the mozzarella cheese, mix well and sprinkle half of the cheese evenly over the top. Put the remaining vegetable mixture into the casserole and sprinkle the remaining cheese on the top. Combine all other ingredients and mix well. Pour the frothy egg mixture over the casserole. Bake in preheated oven, uncovered, for 30 minutes.

Kaki, my fabulous mother, gave me this recipe. She warned me not to add more of any ingredient than is called for in the recipe or it would be too runny. The last time she made her own Spoof Soufflé she figured if one little zucchini was good, two little zucchini would be better—and one more was one too many.

This recipe can either be served as an entrée or a vegetable side dish. I like it as an entrée for lunch with plain sliced tomatoes garnished with chopped parsley and Sunflower Seed Bread.

EGGS PROVENÇALE

6 large tomatoes, at room temperature
2 tablespoons minced parsley
2 tablespoons unprocessed wheat bran
3 garlic buds, minced
1 teaspoon salt
1/4 teaspoon freshly ground black pepper
6 eggs

1-1/2 teaspoons butter or corn oil margarine
2 tablespoons grated Parmesan cheese

Makes 6 servings
Each serving contains approximately:
1.4 grams of fiber
150 calories

Preheat the oven to 350°. Cut tops off tomatoes carefully. Scoop out pulp and keep to use in a salad or other recipes. Place tomato cups in a greased baking dish. Combine parsley, bran, garlic, salt and pepper and mix well. Spoon this mixture evenly into the 6 tomato cups. Place the filled tomato cups in the preheated oven for 8 minutes. Remove from the oven and break an egg into each cup. Put 1/4 teaspoon butter or margarine on each egg. Put the tomato cups back in the preheated oven for 10 to 15 more minutes, or until the eggs are set. Sprinkle each egg with 1 teaspoon Parmesan cheese and put the tomato cups under the broiler until the tops are lightly browned.

I serve Eggs Provençale for luncheons with Watercress Salad and Cheese Straws.

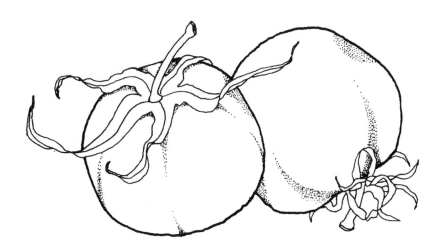

eggs and cheese

CAVIAR CREAMED EGGS

2 cups low-fat milk
3 tablespoons butter or corn oil margarine
1/4 cup whole wheat flour
3/4 teaspoon salt
1/4 teaspoon dry mustard
dash white pepper
1/4 cup fresh lemon juice
6 eggs, hard cooked and finely shredded or
   chopped

1/4 cup finely chopped onion
4 ounces caviar
12 thin slices pumpernickel bread, toasted
watercress or parsley for garnish

Makes 6 servings
Each serving contains approximately:
1.0 gram of fiber
430 calories

Pour the milk in a saucepan and put it on low heat so that it will be at the boiling point when you need it. Melt the butter or margarine in a large saucepan. Add the flour and cook over medium heat, stirring constantly, for 3 minutes. Remove from the heat and add the hot milk, all at once, rapidly stirring with a wire whisk. Put the sauce back on the heat and simmer, stirring constantly, for about 5 minutes or until thickened. Remove from the heat and add the salt, dry mustard and white pepper and mix well. Add the lemon juice, eggs, onion and caviar and again mix well. Spoon the Caviar Creamed Eggs over the pumpernickel toast and garnish with watercress or parsley.

I like to serve Caviar Creamed Eggs for Sunday supper with Cold Buttermilk Borscht in icers to start and whole fresh fruit for dessert.

Variation Serve Caviar Creamed Eggs over Buckwheat Blinis instead of pumpernickel toast.

QUICHE MARY ANN

1 Perfect Bran Pie Crust, unbaked, page 162
8 slices (1/2 pound) bacon, crisply cooked
   and drained
3 cups (3/4 pound) grated Swiss cheese
3 eggs, beaten
1-1/2 cups low-fat milk
1/4 teaspoon salt

1/8 teaspoon freshly ground black pepper

Makes 8 servings
Each serving contains approximately:
.6 gram of fiber
319 calories

Preheat the oven to 350°. Layer the bacon and cheese in the unbaked pie shell. (I always make the pie crust in a 9-inch quiche dish, simply because it looks better.) Start with 1 cup grated cheese, then 4 slices bacon. Follow with 1 more cup of cheese and the remaining 4 slices of bacon and put the last cup of cheese evenly over the top. Beat the eggs with the milk, salt and pepper. Pour this mixture over the cheese and bacon in the pie shell.

Place the quiche on a cookie sheet so that if it bubbles up during baking, it goes on the cookie sheet rather than on the bottom of the oven. Bake in the preheated oven for 1 hour. Remove from oven and allow to cool for 10 to 15 minutes before slicing.

If you want to freeze the quiche, cool to room temperature and wrap it tightly in aluminum foil. To reheat it, remove the quiche from the freezer 3 to 4 hours before reheating. Then heat in a 350° oven for about 15 minutes. This makes an excellent brunch or light supper entrée. It is also a marvelous hors d'oeuvre. When serving it as an hors d'oeuvre, cut it in small cubes or triangles.

When my book, *The Calculating Cook,* was published, my friends Mary Ann and Dr. Gordon Dickie gave a beautiful party in my honor. It was a wine and cheese party held in the garden of their oceanfront home in Honolulu. Mary Ann served the best quiche I had ever tasted in my life. This recipe is my higher fiber, lower calorie version of her quiche!

101

eggs and cheese

SEE'S SOUFFLÉ-SQUARES

4 eggs, separated
2 teaspoons butter or corn oil margarine, melted
1 cup (1/2 pint) low-fat cottage cheese
1/4 cup whole wheat pastry flour
1/4 teaspoon salt

Makes 6 servings
Each serving contains approximately:
.1 gram of fiber
115 calories

Preheat the oven to 375°. Grease a 7- by 12-inch baking dish and set aside. Put the egg whites in a clean, dry bowl. Put the yolks in another large mixing bowl. Beat the egg whites until stiff, but not dry. Transfer the beater to the yolks (this maneuver saves washing the beaters in between). Beat the yolks until they are light in color. Beat the melted butter or margarine, cottage cheese, flour and salt into the egg yolks. Carefully fold in the beaten egg whites. Spoon the mixture into the greased baking dish and spread evenly.

Bake uncovered in the preheated oven for 20 minutes or until lightly and evenly browned on the top. Remove from the oven and cut into 6 squares. It is easiest to remove the squares from the baking dish with a spatula.

The ingredients in this recipe are almost identical to my recipe for Puffy Pancakes in *The Calculating Cook.* However, the methods for cooking and serving are very different. This innovation took place one weekend at Harry See's ranch in the Napa Valley of California. My sister Cheri forgot to melt the butter in the skillet before adding the pancakes and then could not turn them over because they were hopelessly stuck to the bottom of the frying pan. Harry suggested baking them in the oven to cook the top. The result was so successful that he permanently changed his own preparation of my recipe—so I am sharing his invention with you. It is unusual, attractive *and* delicious.

Harry serves See's Soufflé-Squares for lunch with Cheddar Cheese Sauce and a tossed green salad. I personally like them better for breakfast spread lightly with Date Butter. Try them and use your own favorite topping.

You can also successfully freeze See's Soufflé-Squares. Remove them from the baking dish and cool them to room temperature. Wrap them well so that they are airtight. Place the wrapped squares on a cookie sheet, not overlapping, and freeze them. When frozen they can be stacked for storage. Before serving, thaw completely, wrap in foil and heat in a 300° oven for 15 minutes.

STUFFING FONDUE SOUFFLÉ

4 slices whole wheat bread
1 cup (1/4 pound) grated Monterey Jack
   cheese
1/2 teaspoon salt
1 teaspoon ground sage
1/2 teaspoon thyme
1/8 teaspoon white pepper
4 eggs, lightly beaten

2 cups low-fat milk
1/4 cup minced onion

Makes 4 servings
Each serving contains approximately:
.5 gram of fiber
266 calories

Allow bread to stand out on a counter exposed to the air for several hours, so that it can be easily cubed. Cut the bread in 1/4-inch squares. Arrange one-half of the bread cubes in a flat baking dish. Sprinkle one-half of the cheese evenly over the top of the bread; repeat layers, putting the remaining cheese on top. Then combine all other ingredients and mix them well. Pour the liquid mixture over the cheese and bread in the baking dish. Cover and refrigerate overnight. Remove from the refrigerator 2 hours before cooking. To cook, set the baking dish in a shallow pan of cold water and place it in a cold oven. Set the oven for 300° and cook for 1 hour. Check to make sure it is not getting too brown.

    This is a delightfully different substitute for traditional turkey dressing. It is also good served with leftover cold sliced turkey and Curried Cranberry Sauce.

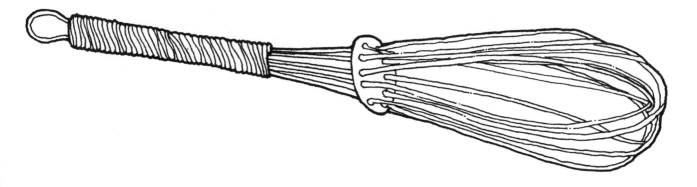

eggs and cheese

BRAN-BRIE PIE

1/4 cup thinly sliced almonds
1 Perfect Bran Pie Crust, page 162, baked
1 pound brie, cubed

Makes 8 servings as an entrée
Each serving contains approximately:
.7 gram of fiber
293 calories

Preheat the oven to 300°. Place the thinly sliced almonds on a cookie sheet in the preheated oven for 10 to 15 minutes or until a golden brown. Watch carefully as they burn easily. Set aside.

Arrange the cubed brie evenly in the baked pie crust. Place the pie in the preheated oven for about 5 minutes or until brie is slightly melted. Remove pie from the oven and sprinkle the toasted almond flakes evenly over the top.

Bran-Brie Pie is one of my favorite luncheon entrées. I serve it with Watercress Salad, leaving the pine nuts off of the salad (they are too much with the almonds on the Bran-Brie Pie). I also like it served with fresh fruit, especially pears! For an hors d'oeuvre, cut the pie into tiny wedges and keep it in a chafing dish or over a hot plate to keep it warm. Your guests will rave about your culinary prowess!

HUBERT'S SUNDAY SANDWICH

2 slices whole grain bread, toasted (Wheat Berry Bread, page 135, is best)
2 tablespoons mayonnaise (Fabulous Mayonnaise, page 54, is best)
1 medium or 1/2 large apple, cored and thinly sliced
1 small, sweet red onion, thinly sliced

2 2-ounce slices Port Salut cheese
2 parsley sprigs, for garnish (optional)

Makes 2 sandwiches
Each serving contains approximately:
1.6 grams of fiber
327 calories

Spread each slice of toasted bread with 1 tablespoon mayonnaise. Spread the sliced apples and onion evenly over the 2 slices. Place the slice of cheese on top and garnish each open-faced sandwich with a sprig of parsley.

Hubert Latimer invented this unusual and delicious sandwich years ago when he was a fashion designer in California. He is now living in New York, still a fabulous designer and still serving this sandwich to guests who drop by on Sundays! The only thing about this sandwich I disagree with Hubert about is that he serves it with red wine and I think it is better served with cold, dry white wine.

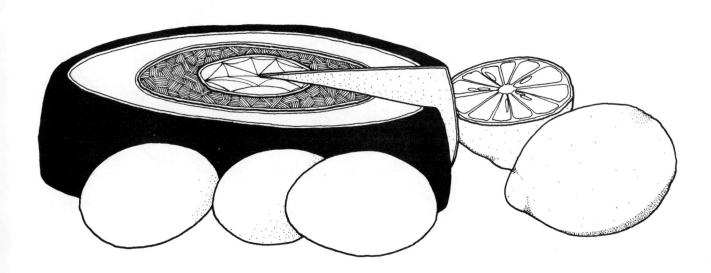

seafood, poultry and meat

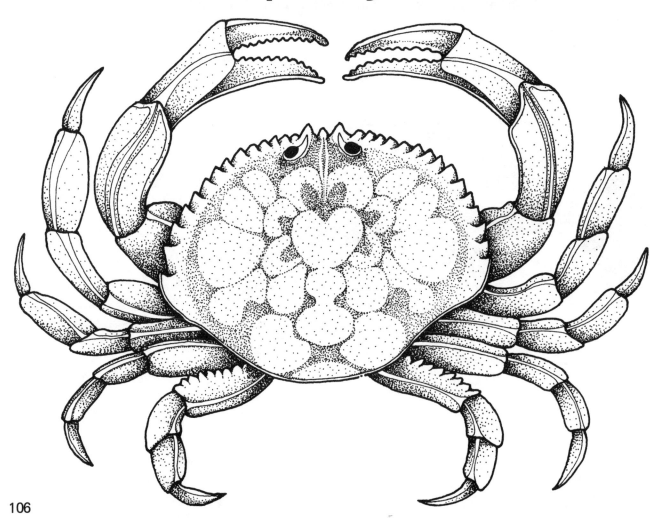

Fish is one of the best sources of protein in our diet. It contains less fat and fewer calories than other animal proteins. Another decided advantage to fish and seafood as major food sources is that they do not take up valuable land space which can be used for growing other crops also essential to our diet. Nor do they eat food which otherwise could be used to feed people. Fish farming is practiced extensively today in the Orient and may well become one of the major sources of animal protein in the future.

If you don't think you like fish, the chances are that you have never had it prepared properly, never had really *fresh* fish—or maybe both! With modern transportation it is possible to buy fresh fish almost everywhere. Find a good fish market or buy good fresh-frozen fish. Frozen fish can be very good if it is thawed properly in cold water. Never cook fish while it is still frozen or it will be tasteless and fall apart while cooking. After properly thawing frozen fish, prepare it in the same manner described in each of my recipes for fresh fish. I always prepare more fish and seafood than I plan to serve because I love to have enough left over for a salad the next day.

Both chicken and the white meat of turkey are highly recommended for low fat diets. Always serve poultry without skin if you are trying to lower the fat and calories.

Chicken is perfect to use in all sorts of exotic recipes because its delicate flavor lends itself equally well to all seasonings. It is also marvelous for parties, because chicken dishes can usually be made ahead of time and reheated successfully.

Red meat contains greater amounts of animal fat than either fish or chicken. For this reason it is usually advisable to limit the amount of red meat served each week if you are trying to lose weight or are on a low-cholesterol, low-saturated fat diet.

Regardless of your personal diet program, I would suggest "common-sense portion-control" when serving steaks. In many restaurants I have been served a steak so large it does not even fit on the serving plate. Few people can eat that much steak at one meal and no one should!

When buying meat, always buy the leanest cut available. Then, before cooking the meat, carefully remove all visible fat. When broiling meat, use a slotted broiling pan or a charcoal barbecue so that the fat can drip off the meat during the cooking. When preparing any boiled meat, such as stew, chill overnight and skim off all fat which forms on the top before reheating and serving. When making gravies from your roasts, always use Defatted Drippings.

The recipes in this section are unusual combinations of fish, poultry or meat and high fiber ingredients.

seafood, poultry and meat

POACHED SALMON ON DILLED WHEAT

4 cups Court Bouillon, page 26
1 2-pound piece fresh salmon
1 tablespoon butter or corn oil margarine
1/2 cup finely chopped onion
4 teaspoons dill seed
1/2 teaspoon salt
4 cups cooked cracked wheat (bulgur)

1 cup finely chopped chives or green
  onion tops
chopped dill or parsley for garnish

Makes 8 servings
Each serving contains approximately:
1.1 grams of fiber
310 calories

Bring the Court Bouillon to a slow boil. Wrap a large piece of cheesecloth around the salmon so that it can be lifted out of the liquid easily in one piece when it is done. Lower the salmon into the simmering bouillon and cook for about 25 minutes.

While the salmon is poaching, melt the butter or margarine in a large skillet. Add the onion and cook, covered, for 5 minutes. Add the dill seed and salt and mix well. Add the cooked cracked wheat and again mix well. Cook, stirring frequently, until the entire mixture is hot. Add the chopped chives and mix well.

Arrange the dilled wheat on a serving platter. Carefully remove the salmon from the cheesecloth and place it on top of the dilled wheat. Garnish the platter with fresh dill or parsley.

This recipe is equally good served cold. If you plan to serve it cold you do not need to heat the dish after adding the cooked cracked wheat. Just mix it thoroughly with the cooked onions, dill seed and salt and refrigerate it until cold. Poach the salmon ahead of time and refrigerate it. Then serve it exactly the same way—this is one of the few recipes that works equally well for hot or cold buffet!

BANANAFISH DISH

1-1/2 pounds firm white fish (I like sea bass or
  red snapper)
2 lemons
salt
2 tablespoons hulled sesame seeds
4 bananas, cut in half lengthwise
3 tablespoons corn oil
1/4 cup Date Syrup, page 49

1/2 teaspoon salt
3 cups hot cooked brown rice

Makes 8 servings
Each serving contains approximately:
.6 gram of fiber
352 calories

If possible, always buy fresh fish. When it is necessary to use frozen fish, allow it to thaw completely before preparation. Wash the fish in cold water and pat dry. Place in a flat glass baking dish and squeeze juice of 1 lemon on the fish and lightly salt. Turn the fish over and squeeze juice of remaining lemon on it and again lightly salt. Cover the dish tightly with aluminum foil or lid and place in the refrigerator.

Preheat the oven to 350°. Place the sesame seeds on a cookie sheet in the preheated oven for about 10 minutes or until a golden brown. Watch carefully as they burn easily. Set aside.

When you are ready to cook the fish, remove it from the refrigerator, allowing enough time for the dish to come to room temperature so that it will not break in the oven. Place the halved bananas on top of the fish. Combine the corn oil, Date Syrup, salt and toasted sesame seeds. Mix well by shaking in a jar with a tight-fitting lid, and pour over the fish and bananas. Tightly cover the dish and place it in a preheated 350° oven for 15 to 20 minutes. Remove the cooked fish from the oven and serve it on the hot rice. Spoon the liquid from the baking dish over the top of each serving.

I named this recipe for Salingers's short story, "A Perfect Day for Bananafish." I love his book, *Nine Stories,* in which it appears. I hope you will love the recipe his title inspired.

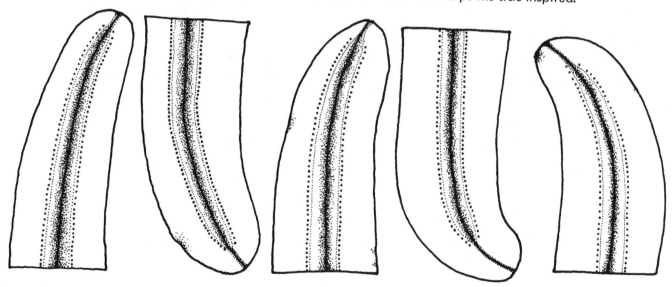

seafood, poultry and meat

TUNA TREAT

1 tablespoon butter or corn oil margarine
1 7-ounce can water-pack tuna, drained
2 large onions, thinly sliced
1/2 teaspoon salt
2 cups cooked short-grain brown rice
1 cup grated Monterey Jack cheese

Makes 4 servings
Each serving contains approximately:
.6 gram of fiber
283 calories

Melt the butter or margarine in a large, heavy iron skillet. Add the drained tuna and sliced onions. Cook over medium heat until the onions are lightly browned, stirring frequently. Add the salt and rice and mix thoroughly. Sprinkle the grated cheese evenly over the top and cover the pan until the cheese has completely melted. This is easy to make and amazingly good to eat. Children love it and they can make it themselves.

SALMON-ANCHOVY ASPIC

1 scant tablespoon (1 envelope) unflavored
   gelatin
1/4 cup dry white wine (I like Chablis)
3/4 cup chicken stock, boiling
3/4 cup ice water
1 teaspoon fresh lemon juice
1/2 teaspoon Worcestershire sauce
1 tablespoon tarragon vinegar
1/4 teaspoon salt
1/8 teaspoon white pepper
2 cups cooked flaked salmon

6 anchovy fillets, finely chopped
2 tablespoons minced onion
1/2 cup finely chopped celery
2 tablespoons unprocessed wheat bran
shredded lettuce or grated cucumber
Dilled Onions Lautrec, page 78

Makes 4 servings
Each serving contains approximately:
.7 gram of fiber
172 calories

Combine the gelatin and the white wine. Allow the gelatin to soften, then add the boiling chicken stock and stir until completely dissolved. Refrigerate and chill until very firm.

When firm, put into a blender with the ice water, lemon juice, Worcestershire sauce, tarragon vinegar, salt and pepper. Blend until frothy. Pour the frothy mixture into a bowl and let stand until mixture starts to thicken. Fold in remaining ingredients, except lettuce and onions.

Pour into an oiled 6-cup fish-shaped mold, if you have one. If not, any oiled mold will do, or use 4 individual molds. Chill all day or overnight before serving. Unmold carefully on a bed of shredded lettuce or grated cucumber and garnish with Dilled Onions Lautrec. I serve Fresh Dill Sauce on the side and toasted Sunflower Seed Bread.

111

seafood, poultry and meat

EGYPTIAN BAKED FISH

1-1/2 pounds firm, fresh fish (halibut or bass
   is excellent)
2 lemons
salt
2 tablespoons olive oil
2 large onions, thinly sliced
3 garlic buds, chopped
1 cup finely chopped celery, without leaves
1 small eggplant, diced
1-1/2 cups tomato sauce

1/2 teaspoon salt
1/2 teaspoon ground cumin
1/4 teaspoon freshly ground black pepper
1 large tomato, sliced
3 cups hot Crunchy Cracked Wheat, page 87

Makes 6 servings
Each serving contains approximately:
1.9 grams of fiber
364 calories

If possible, always buy fresh fish. When it is necessary to use frozen fish, allow it to thaw completely before preparation. Wash the fish in cold water and pat dry. Place in a flat glass baking dish, squeeze juice of 1 lemon on the fish and lightly salt. Turn the fish over and squeeze juice of remaining lemon on it; again lightly salt. Cover the dish tightly with aluminum foil or lid and place in the refrigerator until you are ready to cook it. When you are ready to cook the fish, remove from the refrigerator, allowing enough time for the baking dish to come to room temperature so that the dish will not break in the oven. Preheat the oven to 350°.

Heat the oil in a heavy iron skillet. Add the onions and garlic and cook over medium heat until the onion is lightly browned. Add the celery and eggplant and cook for 5 more minutes. Add the tomato sauce, salt, cumin and pepper. Continue cooking until most of the moisture has been absorbed, about 5 minutes. Remove from heat. Spread the sauce over the fish in the baking dish and arrange the tomato slices evenly over the top. Cover the dish tightly with aluminum foil. Place the covered dish in the preheated oven for about 20 minutes. Remove the cover and cook for 5 more minutes.

Serve each portion over 1/2 cup hot Crunchy Cracked Wheat. I like this recipe served with Watercress Salad.

CRAB CURRY ON COCONUT RICE

3 tablespoons butter or corn oil margarine
4 cups finely chopped onions
1/3 cup whole wheat flour
1 tablespoon curry powder
1/2 teaspoon ground ginger
1 teaspoon salt
1/8 teaspoon white pepper
1 cup chicken stock, boiling
3 cups low-fat milk, heated
1 pound cooked crab meat, diced

1 teaspoon fresh lemon juice
4 cups hot cooked brown rice
1 cup shredded unsweetened coconut
1 cup finely chopped or crushed pineapple

Makes 8 servings
Each serving contains approximately:
1.3 grams of fiber
438 calories

Melt the butter or margarine in a large saucepan or soup kettle. Add the chopped onion and cook, covered, for 5 minutes. Add the flour, curry powder, ginger, salt and white pepper and mix well. Continue cooking, stirring constantly, for 3 minutes. Add the boiling chicken stock and stir rapidly with a wire whisk. Slowly add the hot milk, continuing to stir constantly. Cook slowly, stirring frequently until the sauce has thickened slightly, about 45 minutes. Add the diced crab and lemon juice and heat through.

While the crab is heating combine the brown rice, coconut and pineapple. Serve the Crab Curry over the rice mixture.

The beauty of this curry recipe is that you do not need to serve condiments. The coconut and pineapple in the rice add just the right amount of sweetness to balance the flavor of the curry. I serve this dish with cold Orange Soup to start and a green salad sprinkled with toasted pine nuts. Frozen Bonbons are good for dessert.

seafood, poultry and meat

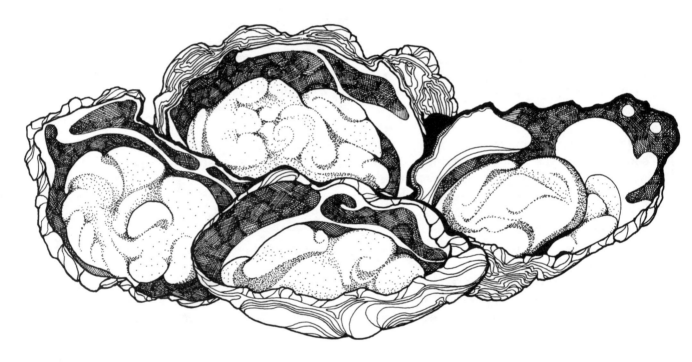

OYSTER CEVICHE

20 fresh oysters in the shell
3 tablespoons fresh lime juice
1 garlic bud, pressed
1/2 teaspoon salt
1/4 teaspoon freshly ground black pepper
1/2 cup finely chopped onion
1 large tomato, finely chopped
1 tablespoon finely chopped pimiento

1/4 cup finely chopped parsley or cilantro
2 tablespoons red wine vinegar
1 teaspoon oregano

Makes 8 servings
Each serving contains approximately:
.2 gram of fiber
44 calories

Remove the oysters from their shells. Wash the shells and set them aside to use for serving the ceviche. Cut the oysters in small pieces and put them in a non-metal container. Pour the lime juice over the oysters and mix in the garlic, salt and pepper. Cover and refrigerate for 24 hours. Four hours before serving add all remaining ingredients and again refrigerate, until you are ready to serve.

To serve the ceviche, place 5 clean oyster half-shells on each of 8 plates. Fill each half-shell with a spoonful of ceviche. I like to serve this as an appetizer, with the half-shells on plates of crushed ice, accompanied with Toasted Tortilla Triangles.

TARRAGON TUNA MOUSSE IN TOMATO BOWLS

1 scant tablespoon (1 envelope) unflavored
   gelatin
1/2 cup dry white wine (I like Chablis)
1 cup well-drained water-packed tuna
1 cup plain yogurt
2 tablespoons unprocessed wheat bran
1 tablespoon tarragon vinegar
1 teaspoon tarragon
1 tablespoon grated onion
1 teaspoon fresh lemon juice
1/2 teaspoon Worcestershire sauce

1/4 teaspoon salt
1/8 teaspoon white pepper
4 large tomatoes
parsley for garnish

Makes 4 servings
Each serving contains approximately:
.7 gram of fiber
172 calories

Sprinkle the gelatin over the wine in a saucepan. Stir over low heat 3 to 4 minutes or until gelatin is completely dissolved. Combine the tuna, yogurt, bran and gelatin mixture and mix well. Add all other ingredients except tomatoes and garnish and mix well. Pour into a bowl and refrigerate all day or overnight before serving.

Slice the tops of the tomatoes off and hollow out each one with a spoon making 4 tomato bowls. Turn the tomatoes upside down to drain thoroughly. Spoon the mousse into the tomato bowls. Garnish with parsley.

I like Green Goddess Dressing spooned over the top of each serving.

seafood, poultry and meat

ZARZUELA
(Spanish Shellfish Stew)

2 small raw lobsters
12 clams in the shell, thoroughly scrubbed
12 mussels in the shell, thoroughly scrubbed
   (if unavailable, use 24 clams in all)
12 medium shrimp in the shell, deveined
12 scallops, cut in half
2 tablespoons olive oil
1 cup finely chopped onion
2 garlic buds, finely chopped
1 small green bell pepper, seeded and finely
   chopped
6 medium tomatoes, peeled and finely diced
1/2 cup whole almonds

1 bay leaf, crushed
1/4 teaspoon powdered saffron
1 teaspoon salt
1/8 teaspoon freshly ground black pepper
3 cups water
1/2 cup dry white wine
1 tablespoon fresh lemon juice
3 tablespoons pernod

Makes 6 servings
Each serving contains approximately:
1.3 grams of fiber
453 calories

Cut each lobster into 3 pieces, leaving the shell attached. Scrub the clams and mussels with a stiff brush until they are *very clean.* Shell the shrimp leaving the tails attached. Using a small sharp knife, make a shallow slit down the back of each shrimp and lift out the intestinal vein. If it does not all come out in one piece, use the point of the knife to scrape out any remaining portions of the vein. Then wash out the incision well with cold water. Cut each scallop in half and wash in cold water. Set all seafood aside.

   In a heavy 8-quart flameproof casserole heat the olive oil. Add the onion, garlic and bell pepper and cook, stirring frequently, 5 minutes or until vegetables are tender but not brown.

   Put 1 cup of the diced tomatoes and the almonds in the blender and blend until smooth. Add the puréed tomato-almond mixture to the onion mixture. Add the remaining tomatoes, bay leaf, saffron, salt and pepper and cook over medium-high heat, stirring constantly until most of the liquid is absorbed.

   Add the water, wine and lemon juice and bring to a boil. Mix well and add the lobster, clams and mussels. Cover the pot and reduce heat to medium low and cook for 10 minutes. Add the shrimp and scallops. Recover and continue cooking for 5 more minutes. Discard any clams or mussels that have not opened.

Just before serving, add the pernod and mix well. Serve in large soup or gumbo bowls with coarse whole grain bread and a tossed green salad. When spooning the zarzuela into the bowls be sure each serving contains an equal amount of each shellfish. Otherwise you will have one or more unhappy guests *and* the calorie count will not be accurate.

Zarzuela is the Spanish counterpart of the French bouillabaisse and the Italian (San Francisco) cioppino. All are hearty seafood stews. Since I have recipes for cioppino and bouillabaisse in my other cookbooks, I decided to put a recipe for zarzuela in this one!

SHRIMP KASHA

1/2 cup pine nuts
2 tablespoons butter or corn oil margarine
1 cup finely chopped onion
1 cup (1/2 pound) kasha (buckwheat groats)
1 egg, lightly beaten
1/2 teaspoon salt
3/4 teaspoon ground nutmeg
1/2 teaspoon ground sage

2-1/2 cups chicken stock, boiling
2 pounds cleaned cooked shrimp (6 cups)
1/2 cup raisins

Makes 8 servings
Each serving contains approximately:
.5 gram of fiber
343 calories

Preheat the oven to 350°. Place the pine nuts on a cookie sheet in the preheated oven for approximately 10 minutes or until a golden brown. Watch carefully as they burn easily. Set aside.

Melt butter or margarine in a skillet. Add onion and cook until clear and tender, about 5 minutes. Combine kasha, egg, salt, nutmeg and sage in another pan. Cook over medium heat stirring occasionally until kasha becomes dry, about 5 minutes. Combine onion and kasha mixtures with the hot chicken stock. Cook, covered, over low heat for about 30 minutes, or until all liquid is absorbed. Add shrimp, raisins and toasted pine nuts. Mix well and heat through.

I like Shrimp Kasha served with Brussels Sprouts in Herb Butter and Bran-Mango Mousse for dessert.

seafood, poultry and meat

BLINI AU CAVIAR

24 Buckwheat Blini, page 149
1 cup sour cream
8 ounces caviar (fresh beluga or the best
   your budget will allow!)
1/4 cup minced onion
3 hard-cooked eggs, minced or shredded

Makes 6 servings
Each serving contains approximately:
.3 gram of fiber
312 calories

Spread each Buckwheat Blini with 2 teaspoons sour cream. Place 2 teaspoons of caviar on top of the sour cream. Sprinkle each blini evenly with the 1/2 teaspoon minced onion and shredded hard-cooked egg.

This is the classic presentation for caviar and it is also my favorite. Fresh beluga caviar is the most highly acclaimed of all appetizers and justly so. To caviar lovers, it is the ultimate taste treat in the world. However, it is also the most expensive. I have served this recipe with relatively inexpensive lumpfish caviar, elegantly presented, and received raves from my guests.

This is also a fabulous and most unusual luncheon entrée. When serving it for luncheons I serve 4 blinis per person with Watercress Salad and fresh fruit for dessert.

BRAN-BREADED SNAILS
(The High Fiber Approach to Escargots)

18 snails, well washed
2 cups water
1 bay leaf
1 tablespoon finely chopped parsley
1/8 teaspoon thyme
1/8 teaspoon ground allspice
2 garlic buds, crushed
1/4 teaspoon salt
1 cup unprocessed wheat bran

1/2 teaspoon salt
1/8 teaspoon white pepper
2 tablespoons corn oil
fresh lemon juice or lemon wedges

Makes 18 snails
Each snail contains approximately:
.5 gram of fiber
45 calories

Put the washed snails in a saucepan and add the water. Add bay leaf, parsley, thyme, allspice, garlic and salt. Bring to a boil, immediately reduce heat and simmer for 10 minutes. While the snails are cooking, combine the bran, salt and white pepper and mix well. Remove the snails from the water and roll in the bran mixture until each snail is completely covered. Heat the oil in a heavy cured iron skillet and cook the snails until lightly browned. Sprinkle the snails with lemon juice before serving or serve with lemon wedges.

These snails may be served as an hors d'oeuvre, appetizer or entrée. I like them best as an entrée served with Kaki's Spoof Soufflé and a big green salad.

seafood, poultry and meat

ARABIAN CHICKEN PILAF

1/2 cup pine nuts
2 teaspoons corn oil
1 cup finely chopped onion
1/4 teaspoon ground allspice
1/4 teaspoon ground nutmeg
1/4 teaspoon ground cinnamon
3 cups chopped cooked chicken, in fairly
    large pieces

1/2 cup raisins
3 cups cooked brown rice

Makes 6 servings
Each serving contains approximately:
.7 gram of fiber
331 calories

Preheat the oven to 325°. Place the pine nuts in the preheated oven for 10 to 15 minutes or until a golden brown color. Watch carefully as they burn easily. Remove from the oven and set aside.

Heat the corn oil in a cured heavy iron skillet and add the onion. Cook, stirring frequently, until the onion is cooked, about 15 minutes. Add the allspice, nutmeg and cinnamon to the onion and mix well. Remove from heat, add the pine nuts, chicken, raisins and cooked rice and mix thoroughly. Pour entire mixture into a casserole, cover and place in the preheated oven for 20 minutes. Remove from the oven and leave covered until ready to serve.

You can make this ahead and reheat it before serving. If you are making it ahead of time, I suggest putting it in a casserole to refrigerate. Then to reheat, bring it to room temperature and put it in a 325° oven for about 30 minutes or until heated through.

I like to serve a lettuce salad with Fruit Salad Dressing with this entrée.

LEBANESE POULTRY PILAF

2 tablespoons olive oil
2 medium onions, chopped
1 cup cracked wheat (bulgur)
2 cups chicken stock
1-1/2 teaspoons salt
1 teaspoon ground allspice
1/2 teaspoon ground nutmeg
1/4 teaspoon freshly ground black pepper
dash cayenne pepper

3 cups chopped cooked turkey or chicken,
    in fairly large pieces
1 teaspoon fresh lemon juice

Makes 6 servings
Each serving contains approximately:
.7 gram of fiber
346 calories

Heat the olive oil in a large heavy iron skillet. Add the chopped onions and the cracked wheat. Cook over medium heat, stirring frequently, until the onion is lightly browned. Add the chicken stock and all seasonings. Mix well and bring to a boil. Cover, reduce heat and simmer for 30 minutes or until chicken stock is absorbed. Then add the turkey or chicken and lemon juice. Mix well and heat through.

I serve my Lebanese Poultry Pilaf with Spinach Salad, a dollop of plain yogurt and peta bread for a real Middle Eastern meal.

ORIENTAL PEANUT CHICKEN SUEY

1/4 cup soy sauce
2 teaspoons date "sugar"
2 teaspoons grated fresh ginger root, or
1 teaspoon ground ginger
2 whole chicken breasts, boned, skinned and cut in 1-inch strips
2 tablespoons peanut oil
1 cup sliced mushrooms
1 cup water
3/4 cup finely sliced green onion tops
1/2 cup chopped bamboo shoots
1/2 cup sliced water chestnuts

2 tablespoons water
1 tablespoon cornstarch
1 pound fresh spinach leaves
1 cup dry roasted peanuts
3 cups hot cooked brown rice

Makes 6 servings
Each serving contains approximately:
2.0 grams of fiber
316 calories

Combine soy sauce, date sugar and ginger. Add the chicken and allow to stand for 10 minutes.

Heat peanut oil in a large skillet with a lid over high heat. Add chicken and soy sauce mixture to the hot peanut oil and stir constantly until chicken is well browned. Reduce heat and add mushrooms, water, green onion tops, bamboo shoots and water chestnuts. Cover and simmer for 5 minutes.

Combine the 2 tablespoons of water with the 1 tablespoon of cornstarch and mix until cornstarch is completely dissolved. Add the cornstarch mixture to the chicken and vegetables and mix well. Add the spinach leaves (leaving them whole if they are young and tender) and again cover and cook for 5 minutes. Remove the pan from the heat and add the peanuts. Mix well and serve over brown rice.

Serve Oriental Peanut Chicken Suey with cooked bean sprouts and Bran-Mango Mousse for dessert. Your guests will love this deliciously different, light meal.

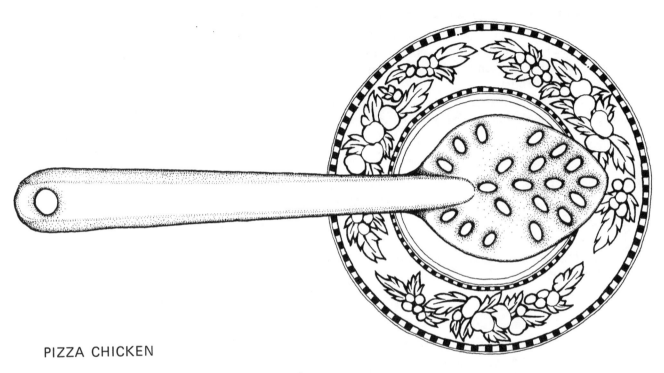

PIZZA CHICKEN

2 cups tomato juice
2 tablespoons red wine vinegar
1/4 cup unprocessed wheat bran
1/4 teaspoon salt
1 medium onion, thinly sliced
1 teaspoon oregano
4 whole chicken breasts, boned, halved,
    skinned and all visible fat removed
1 tablespoon butter or corn oil margarine

salt
freshly ground black pepper
1/2 cup chicken stock
1 cup grated mozzarella cheese

Makes 8 servings
Each serving contains approximately:
.6 gram of fiber
293 calories

Put the tomato juice in a large saucepan. Add the vinegar, bran, salt and onion and mix thoroughly. Bring the mixture to a boil and reduce the heat. Simmer uncovered for 1 hour. Add the oregano and continue to simmer uncovered for 30 minutes.

    Preheat the oven to 400°. Put the chicken breasts in a baking dish large enough not to overlap them. Rub a little butter or corn oil margarine evenly on each piece of chicken, then sprinkle salt and freshly ground black pepper over the tops. Pour the chicken stock in the baking dish. Cover the dish tightly with a lid or aluminum foil and place it in the preheated oven for 20 minutes.

Remove the chicken from the oven and pour off the liquid. Spread the tomato sauce evenly over the chicken and place it back in the oven, uncovered, for 10 minutes. Remove from the oven and sprinkle the grated cheese evenly over the chicken. Place it under the broiler until the cheese is melted and lightly browned.

Serve Pizza Chicken with a green salad with Italian Fiber Dressing, Fettuccini al Jeanno and fresh fruit for dessert.

SHERRIED CHICKEN AND MUSHROOMS ON RICE

2 tablespoons butter or corn oil margarine
1 pound mushrooms, sliced (4 cups)
3 whole chicken breasts, boned, halved,
   skinned and all visible fat removed
salt
white pepper
1 tablespoon butter or corn oil margarine
1/4 cup chicken stock

1/2 cup sherry
3 cups hot cooked brown rice

Makes 6 servings
Each serving contains approximately:
.8 gram of fiber
261 calories

Preheat oven to 400°. Melt the 2 tablespoons butter or margarine in a large pan. Add the mushrooms and cook until just tender.

Place the boned breasts in a flat baking dish just large enough to hold them. Sprinkle lightly with salt and white pepper. Put 1/2 teaspoon of butter or margarine over each breast, rubbing it into the surface with the back of a spoon. Combine the chicken stock and sherry and pour over the chicken breasts. Spoon the mushrooms evenly over the top of the dish. Cover dish tightly with aluminum foil and place in the preheated oven for 25 to 30 minutes. Do not overcook or chicken will be dry. Put the hot rice on a serving platter. Place the cooked chicken breasts on top of the rice and spoon the mushrooms and juices in the baking dish evenly over the top of the chicken.

If you want to make this dish ahead of time put it in a large casserole instead of a serving platter. Cover and refrigerate. Before serving bring to room temperature and place covered in a 325° oven for 25 minutes or until thoroughly heated.

seafood, poultry and meat

CHICKEN MOLE

1 3-1/2-pound whole frying chicken
salt
1 tablespoon corn oil
2 garlic buds, minced
1 medium onion, finely chopped
2 large tomatoes, peeled and diced
1/4 cup finely chopped raisins
1/4 cup chopped cilantro (or 1 tablespoon
    dried)
5 tablespoons chili powder
4 tablespoons unhomogenized peanut butter
1/4 cup carob powder, firmly packed
2 tablespoons unprocessed wheat bran

1 teaspoon date "sugar"
1-1/2 teaspoons salt
1/2 teaspoon ground cumin
1/2 teaspoon ground cinnamon
1/4 teaspoon ground cloves
1/4 teaspoon aniseed
3 cups chicken stock, heated

Makes 8 servings
Each serving contains approximately:
.5 gram of fiber
175 calories

Preheat the oven to 350°. Put the chicken, breast side down, in a flat roasting or baking dish and salt it lightly. Bake in the preheated oven for about 1 hour or until the liquid runs clear when the chicken is tipped. Remove chicken from the oven and allow to cool until it can easily be handled. Remove the skin and all visible fat. Cut the meat from the bones leaving it in fairly large pieces. Set chicken aside to add to mole sauce.

While chicken is roasting make the sauce. Heat the oil in a cured heavy iron skillet. Combine all other ingredients except chicken stock and mix thoroughly. Put the mixture in the skillet and cook, stirring constantly, over medium heat for 10 minutes. Add the hot chicken stock to the mixture and mix well. Simmer uncovered over low heat for 30 minutes, stirring occasionally. Add the roasted chicken pieces to the mole sauce and mix well, or pass the chicken and let each person spoon the mole sauce over the chicken.

This is my favorite Mexican dish. It is also good made with leftover turkey—a "super supper" after the holidays. Serve it with Christmas Rice, plenty of hot tortillas, crisp green salad with Mexican Fiber Dressing and fresh fruit for dessert. *Ole!*

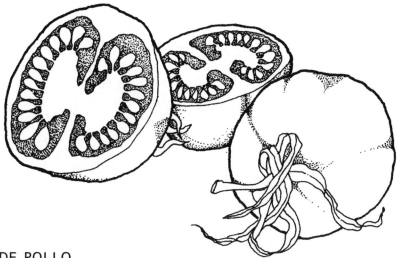

ENCHILADAS DE POLLO

1 tablespoon corn oil
1 large onion, chopped
1-1/2 teaspoons salt
1 tablespoon chili powder
1/2 teaspoon ground cumin
3 medium tomatoes, peeled and diced
2 cups chopped cooked chicken
1/2 cup chicken stock

1-1/2 cups grated sharp cheddar cheese
8 corn tortillas, warmed

Makes 8 enchiladas
Each enchilada contains approximately:
.7 gram of fiber
221 calories

Preheat oven to 350°. Heat the oil in a skillet. Add the chopped onion and cook until tender. Add the salt, chili powder and cumin and mix well. Add the tomatoes, chicken and chicken stock, mix well and cook for 5 minutes on low heat.

Add 3/4 cup of the grated cheese to the mixture and mix thoroughly. Spoon the enchilada mixture evenly down the center of each tortilla. Roll the warm tortilla around the warm cheese mixture and place, seam side down, in a greased 7- by 12-inch baking dish. Spoon any remaining sauce over the enchiladas in the dish evenly and sprinkle the remaining 3/4 cup of grated cheese over the tops of the 8 enchiladas. Cover the baking dish and bake in the preheated oven for 30 minutes.

Chicken enchiladas are perfect for a marvelous Mexican-style dinner. I start with Gazpacho as an appetizer and serve Frijoles Refritos con Queso with the chicken enchiladas. For dessert I like Garbanzo Bean Cake with fresh fruit.

seafood, poultry and meat

CHILI CON CARNE

1 pound dried kidney beans
1/2 cup wheat berries
6 cups water
2 tablespoons butter or corn oil margarine
1 medium onion, peeled and chopped
2 garlic buds, finely chopped
1/2 cup finely chopped green jalapeño chilies
1-1/2 pounds ground sirloin
1/2 pound bulk pork sausage
1 tablespoon whole wheat flour
3 large tomatoes, chopped and mashed
1/2 cup chopped celery, without leaves
1/4 pound mushrooms, sliced
1/2 cup chopped green bell pepper
1/4 cup finely chopped parsley
3/4 cup chili sauce

1/4 cup date "sugar"
1-1/2 teaspoons salt
1-1/2 teaspoons garlic salt
1/2 teaspoon dry mustard
1/4 teaspoon freshly ground black pepper
1-1/2 tablespoons chopped cilantro
    (or 1-1/2 teaspoons dried)
1-1/2 teaspoons oregano
2 tablespoons chili powder
chopped chives or green onion tops (optional)
yogurt or sour cream (optional)

Makes 12 servings
Each serving contains approximately:
3.5 grams of fiber
339 calories

Wash the beans in cold water and drain completely. Put the wheat berries and beans in a large pot, add the water and soak overnight. To cook, bring the beans to a boil in the same water, reduce heat and simmer for about 2 hours or until tender.

Melt the butter or margarine in a large, cured heavy iron skillet. Add the onion, garlic and chilies and cook until the onion is tender. Add the ground sirloin and cook until medium-well done.

In a separate skillet, cook the sausage meat until done and well-browned. Pour off all of the fat from the sausage and add the sausage to the sirloin. (I put it in a colander to drain.) Add the flour to the meat and mix well. Cook for 10 minutes, stirring frequently. Transfer the meat to a larger soup kettle or Dutch oven. Add tomatoes, celery, mushrooms, bell pepper, parsley, chili sauce and date "sugar" and simmer for 30 minutes. Add all remaining ingredients and simmer for 1 hour and 15 minutes.

This is my favorite chili recipe. It is an adaptation of Mildred Mead's favorite chili which she serves in large bowls with a dollop of sour cream on the top. I serve mine with a scoop of plain yogurt on top and sprinkle each serving generously with chopped chives. I also serve a tossed green salad with Creamy Blue Cheese Dressing and Roughage Rolls.

CUBAN BLACK BEANS

1 pound black beans
6 cups water
2 tablespoons butter or corn oil margarine
1 pound bulk pork sausage
1 medium onion, chopped
3 medium tart green apples, chopped
2 garlic buds, pressed
2 teaspoons salt
1/4 teaspoon freshly ground black pepper
1 teaspoon dry mustard
1 teaspoon chili powder

1/2 cup date "sugar"
1-1/2 cups tomato juice
1/4 cup dark rum
1 cup sour cream
1 cup finely chopped green onion tops

Makes 12 servings
Each serving contains approximately:
2.3 grams of fiber
373 calories

Wash the beans in a colander, then put them in a large pan with a lid. Add 6 cups of water, cover and soak overnight. Add the butter or margarine and bring the beans in the same water to a boil. Reduce heat, cover and simmer until beans are tender, about 2 hours.

While the beans are cooking, put the pork sausage in a skillet and cook on medium heat, stirring frequently until well browned. Then drain the liquid from the pan. Add the cooked sausage to the cooked beans. Add all other ingredients except rum, sour cream and chopped onions. Mix well and bring to a boil. As soon as it reaches a boil, pour the entire mixture into a large casserole and bake in a preheated 325° oven for 2 hours. Five minutes before serving, add the 1/4 cup of dark rum and mix thoroughly.

To serve use large soup or gumbo bowls. Put 4 teaspoons of sour cream on the top of each serving and sprinkle 4 teaspoons of green onion over the top.

This is a variation of a recipe I stole from my good friends Barbara and Ken Nelson years ago. The first time I ever had Cuban Black Beans was at a party in their home. They served them buffet style and let each person put his own sour cream and chopped green onion on the top. It is good with a tossed green salad and toasted Roughage Rolls. The Nelsons recommend serving a California Zinfandel with Cuban Black Beans.

seafood, poultry and meat

PUERTO RICAN KIDNEY BEANS

1 pound dried kidney beans
6 cups water
1 green bell pepper, halved and seeded
1 medium onion, halved
2 bay leaves
2 tablespoons corn oil
2 cups diced cooked ham
1 cup tomato sauce
2 garlic buds, chopped

1-1/2 teaspoons salt
1/2 teaspoon freshly ground black pepper
1 tablespoon oregano

Makes 8 servings
Each serving contains approximately:
2.9 grams of fiber
318 calories

Wash the kidney beans in a colander. Put the washed beans in a large pan with a lid. Add the water, bell pepper, onion and bay leaves and bring to a boil. Reduce the heat and simmer the beans, covered, until they are tender, about 2 hours. While the beans are cooking, heat the corn oil in a heavy iron skillet. Add the ham and cook, stirring frequently, until browned. Set aside.

When the beans are tender, remove the bell pepper and onion from the pot and put them in a blender. Add the tomato sauce, garlic, salt, pepper and oregano to the blender and blend until smooth. Pour the contents of the blender into the pan with the ham and simmer for 10 minutes. Then pour it into the beans and simmer for 30 minutes.

My nutritional consultant, Taita Pearn, was raised in Puerto Rico. This is her own very favorite Puerto Rican recipe and it is delicious. She recommends serving it with Fluffy Brown Rice and a green salad. I like it even better with Brown-Berried Rice.

DAVE'S HASH

2 pounds ground beef
2 medium onions, chopped
2 tablespoons butter or corn oil margarine
1 pound mushrooms, sliced
4 cups Brown-Bran Sauce, page 41

Makes 8 servings
Each serving contains approximately:
1.5 grams of fiber
328 calories

Put the ground beef in a cured heavy iron skillet. Add the chopped onions and cook until the meat is done and onions are tender. In another skillet, melt the butter or margarine and add the sliced mushrooms, cooking the mushrooms until tender. Add the cooked mushrooms to the meat and onions. Then add the Brown-Bran Sauce and mix thoroughly.

seafood, poultry and meat

SHOPPERS STEW

2 pounds lean beef, cubed
6 carrots, cross cut in rounds 1/2 inch thick
5 celery stalks, without leaves, cut in
   1/2-inch pieces
3 potatoes, cut in 1-inch cubes
1-1/2 large onions, chopped
1 green bell pepper, seeded and chopped
2 large tomatoes, chopped and mashed
1 cup tomato sauce
1 tablespoon date "sugar"

1 teaspoon salt
1/4 teaspoon freshly ground black pepper
1 teaspoon Worcestershire sauce
3 tablespoons quick-cooking tapioca

Makes 8 servings
Each serving contains approximately:
1.7 grams of fiber
301 calories

Preheat oven to 250°. Put beef, carrots, celery, potatoes, onions and bell pepper in a large casserole with a lid or a small roasting pan. Mash the tomatoes in a large mixing bowl. Add all remaining ingredients and mix well. Add the tomato mixture to the beef mixture in the casserole and mix well. Cover and bake in the preheated oven for 5 hours.

     Whether you are going shopping for a new ball gown or a lawn mower, chances are that it is going to take you three times longer than you had anticipated. The only problem arises when you return home just in time for dinner and there is no dinner. Your problems are over! Before you leave in the morning put Shoppers Stew in the oven and enjoy your day. Come home late and serve your stew with lettuce wedges covered with Creamy Blue Cheese Dressing and Fabulous Fruit Cake for dessert.

TROPICAL HAM SLICES

8 slices (1 pound) cooked ham, about
   1/8 inch thick
1 cup unsweetened pineapple juice
2 teaspoons cornstarch
1/2 cup unprocessed wheat bran
1/2 teaspoon salt
1/2 teaspoon ground cinnamon
1/8 teaspoon ground cloves

2 bananas
2 cups finely chopped pineapple

Makes 8 servings
Each serving contains approximately:
.8 gram of fiber
216 calories

Preheat oven to 350°. Trim all fat from the ham. Place the ham slices in a flat glass baking dish. Pour the pineapple juice in a saucepan; add cornstarch, bran, salt, cinnamon and cloves. Cook over medium heat until the juice is clear and slightly thickened.

Peel the bananas and cut each one in quarters, first cutting it lengthwise. Place 1/4 banana on top of each slice of ham. Evenly spoon the chopped pineapple over the ham slices. Pour the sauce evenly over the top of the garnished ham. Bake in the preheated oven for 20 minutes.

This is a marvelous meat dish for a Sunday brunch. I like to serve it with Curried Eggs and Orange Bread.

COMPANY LAMB CHOPS

4 loin lamb chops, 1-1/2 inches thick
1 lemon
garlic salt
freshly ground black pepper
1/3 cup Dijon-style mustard
4 teaspoons unprocessed wheat bran

1 cup finely chopped parsley

Makes 4 servings
Each serving contains approximately:
.3 gram of fiber
231 calories

Preheat the oven to 500°. Remove all visible fat from the lamb chops and place them in a flat baking dish. Rub both sides of each chop with lemon. Then sprinkle garlic salt and pepper on both sides of each chop. Combine the mustard, bran and parsley and mix well. Cover each lamb chop with parsley mixture, pressing it down firmly with your hands. Put the lamb chops in the preheated oven for *4 minutes*—then turn the oven *off* and *do not open* the door for 30 minutes.

I call this recipe Company Lamb Chops because it is an ideal dinner entrée for busy people giving dinner parties. You can prepare the lamb chops many hours in advance or even a day ahead of time. Cover them tightly and refrigerate until you are 34 minutes from serving time. Even then if you leave them in a little longer than 30 minutes after the oven is turned off the chops will not be overcooked. I like lamb served a bright pink and that is the way your lamb chops will look using this timing. If you prefer lamb chops well done, bake them for 5 minutes instead of 4 before turning off the oven.

I serve this unusual and delicious dish with Fresh Fruit Salad and Christmas Rice.

breads, pasta, pancakes, cereals

Baking your own bread can be lots of fun and helps greatly in switching to a totally unrefined diet. Unrefined flours not only contain more fiber than white flour but they also have a lower absorption rate and fewer calories, making them ideal for weight-reducing diets. Breads made with unrefined, completely natural ingredients also taste so much better than the white, gummy loaves we all see people pinching in grocery stores.

If you have never made your own pasta, you don't know what you've been missing. Surprise your friends with Fettuccini al Jeanno the next time you entertain.

The pancake recipes in this chapter are among my favorite recipes in the book. The Gingerbread Pancakes make a deliciously different breakfast and they are equally good served for dessert. Leftover, they make great cookies for children's school lunches.

BRAN-RAISIN BREAD

1/2 cup raisins
1-1/2 cups whole bran cereal
1 cup date "sugar"
2-3/4 cups buttermilk
2 eggs, lightly beaten
1 teaspoon baking soda
4 teaspoons baking powder
3 cups whole wheat pastry flour

1/2 teaspoon salt
1 tablespoon vanilla extract

Makes 2 loaves; 16 slices each
Each slice contains approximately:
.6 gram of fiber
73 calories

Soak raisins, whole bran cereal and date "sugar" in the buttermilk for at least 15 minutes. While this mixture is soaking, combine the beaten egg, baking soda and baking powder and mix well. Combine the flour and salt. Add it to the egg mixture and mix well using a large spoon. Add vanilla extract to the soaked raisins, whole bran cereal and date "sugar." Combine with the other ingredients and mix well. Preheat the oven to 350°.

Lightly grease and flour 2 loaf pans. Divide the dough equally between the 2 pans and allow to stand for 20 minutes before baking. Bake in the preheated oven for 1 hour and 15 minutes.

To cool the bread, turn the pans on their sides on a rack. When the bread is cool enough to handle, remove the bread from the pans and continue to cool on the racks. Or it is delicious served hot.

To store bread, cool to room temperature, wrap tightly and refrigerate. To serve the bread, slice it, lightly butter each slice and put the slices back together again. Wrap tightly in aluminum foil and put in a preheated 325° oven for about 15 minutes.

breads, pasta, pancakes, cereals

WHOLE WHEAT BREAD

1-1/2 tablespoons active dry yeast (2 packages)
1 tablespoon date "sugar"
1/4 cup warm water
1/2 cup low-fat milk
2 tablespoons butter or corn oil margarine
2 tablespoons date "sugar"
1/2 teaspoon salt
1 egg, lightly beaten

3 cups whole wheat pastry flour (you add
   3 cups and use a little more for kneading)
butter or corn oil margarine

Makes 1 loaf; 20 slices
Each slice contains approximately:
.5 gram of fiber
75 calories

Combine yeast, the 1 tablespoon of date "sugar" and warm water. Set aside out of a draft and allow to double in bulk. This only takes a few minutes.

While the yeast is rising combine the milk and butter or margarine in a saucepan and heat slowly until the butter has melted. Add 2 tablespoons of date "sugar" and salt to the milk mixture. Combine beaten egg with milk mixture and mix thoroughly.

Combine the milk mixture with the yeast mixture in a large bowl. Add the flour 1 cup at a time, mixing thoroughly. You will have to work the last 1/2 cup of flour in by kneading with your hands. Cover and allow to double in bulk, about 1-1/2 hours.

When the dough has doubled, knead it on a flour-dusted board for 10 minutes or until it is smooth and elastic. Rub the dough ball with butter or margarine. Cover and allow it to rise again until doubled in bulk, about 30 minutes.

Knead again into a loaf shape and place it in a greased loaf pan. Cover and allow to rise until nearly doubled in size, about 30 minutes. Bake in a preheated 325° oven 35 to 40 minutes or until it is a golden brown and sounds hollow when tapped. Rub the top with a little butter or margarine and put back in the oven for about 3 minutes. This glazes the bread and makes it prettier!

Remove bread from oven and allow bread to cool to room temperature on a rack. It is much easier to slice when cool. Even if you want to serve the bread hot, it is better to cool it first, slice it, butter it if desired, wrap it in foil and reheat it.

WHEAT BERRY BREAD

1-1/2 tablespoons active dry yeast (2 packages)
1 tablespoon date "sugar"
1/4 cup warm water
1/2 cup milk
2 tablespoons butter or corn oil margarine
2 tablespoons date "sugar"
1/2 teaspoon salt
1 egg, lightly beaten
1/4 cup wheat berries, soaked in water to cover
 for at least 24 hours and drained

3 cups whole wheat pastry flour (you add
 3 cups and use a little more for kneading)
butter or corn oil margarine

Makes 1 loaf; 20 slices
Each slice contains approximately:
.6 gram of fiber
77 calories

Combine yeast, 1 tablespoon of date "sugar" and warm water. Set aside, out of a draft, and allow to double in bulk. This only takes a few minutes.

While the yeast is rising combine the milk and butter or margarine in a saucepan and heat slowly until the butter has melted. Add the 2 tablespoons of date "sugar" and salt to the milk mixture. Combine beaten egg with milk mixture and mix thoroughly.

Combine the milk mixture with the yeast mixture in a large bowl. Add the wheat berries. Add the flour 1 cup at a time, mixing thoroughly. You will have to work the last 1/2 cup of flour in by kneading with your hands. Cover and allow to double in bulk, about 1-1/2 hours.

When the dough has doubled, knead it on a flour-dusted board for 10 minutes or until it is smooth and elastic. Rub the dough ball with butter or margarine. Cover and allow it to rise again until doubled in bulk, about 30 minutes.

Knead again into a loaf shape and place it in a greased loaf pan. Cover and allow to rise until nearly doubled in size, about 30 minutes. Bake in a preheated 325° oven 35 to 40 minutes or until it is a golden brown and sounds hollow when tapped. Rub the top with a little butter or margarine and put back in the oven for about 3 minutes.

Remove the bread from the oven and allow bread to cool to room temperature on a rack. It is much easier to slice when cool. Even if you want to serve the bread hot, it is better to cool it first, slice it, butter it if desired, wrap it in foil and reheat it.

breads, pasta, pancakes, cereals

SUNFLOWER SEED BREAD

1/2 cup sunflower seeds
1-1/2 tablespoons active dry yeast (2 packages)
1 tablespoon date "sugar"
1/4 cup warm water
1/2 cup milk
2 tablespoons butter or corn oil margarine
2 tablespoons date "sugar"
1/2 teaspoon salt
1 egg, lightly beaten

3 cups whole wheat pastry flour (you add
 3 cups and use a little more for kneading)
butter or corn oil margarine

Makes 1 loaf; 20 slices
Each slice contains approximately:
.6 gram of fiber
85 calories

Preheat the oven to 350°. Place the sunflower seeds on a cookie sheet in the preheated oven for approximately 10 minutes or until a golden brown. Watch carefully as they burn easily. Set aside.

Combine yeast, the 1 tablespoon of date "sugar" and warm water. Set aside, out of a draft, and allow to double in bulk. This only takes a few minutes.

While the yeast is rising combine the milk and butter or margarine in a saucepan and heat slowly until the butter has melted. Add 2 tablespoons of date "sugar" and salt to the milk mixture. Combine beaten egg with milk mixture and mix thoroughly.

Combine the milk mixture with the yeast mixture in a large bowl. Add the toasted sunflower seeds. Add the flour 1 cup at a time, mixing thoroughly, working the last 1/2 cup of flour in by kneading with your hands. Cover and allow to double in bulk, about 1-1/2 hours.

When the dough has doubled, knead it on a flour-dusted board for 10 minutes or until it is smooth and elastic. Rub the dough ball with butter or margarine. Cover and allow it to rise again until doubled in bulk, about 30 minutes.

Knead again into a loaf shape and place it in a greased loaf pan. Cover and allow to rise until nearly doubled in size, about 30 minutes. Bake in a preheated 325° oven 35 to 40 minutes or until it is a golden brown and sounds hollow when tapped. Rub the top with a little butter or margarine and put back in the oven for about 3 minutes.

Remove bread from oven and allow bread to cool to room temperature on a rack. It is much easier to slice when cool. Even if you want to serve the bread hot, it is better to cool it first, slice it, butter it if desired, wrap it in foil and reheat it.

SPICE NUT BREAD

2 cups whole wheat pastry flour
1 tablespoon baking powder
3/4 teaspoon salt
1 teaspoon ground cinnamon
1/2 teaspoon ground allspice
1/2 teaspoon ground nutmeg
1/8 teaspoon ground cloves
2 tablespoons carob powder
4 tablespoons butter or corn oil margarine
3/4 cup date "sugar"

1 teaspoon vanilla extract
2 eggs
1 cup unsweetened applesauce
1/2 cup chopped walnuts

Makes 1 loaf; 20 slices
Each slice contains approximately:
.6 gram of fiber
110 calories

Preheat oven to 350°. Combine flour, baking powder, salt, cinnamon, allspice, nutmeg, cloves and carob powder and set aside. Cream together the butter or margarine, date "sugar" and vanilla extract. Beat in eggs, one at a time. Add applesauce, mix well and set aside for 10 minutes, then slowly stir in the flour mixture. Add the chopped walnuts and mix well.

Spoon dough into a well-greased standard loaf pan and bake in the preheated oven for 1 hour. Remove from the oven and place the pan on its side for 10 minutes, then turn bread out onto a wire rack to cool. This bread is good with fruit salads for lunch or as a breakfast bread.

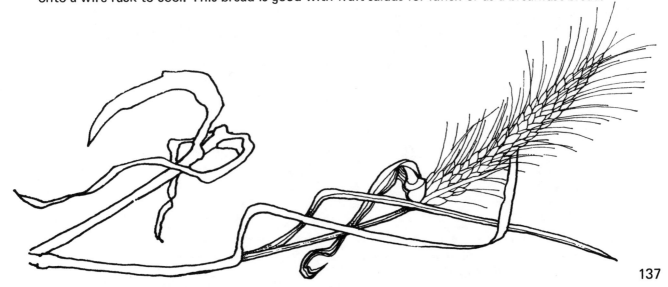

breads, pasta, pancakes, cereals

ORANGE BREAD

1 scant tablespoon active dry yeast (1 package)
1/4 cup fresh orange juice, warmed
1 cup (1/2 pint) small curd cottage cheese
3 tablespoons date "sugar"
1 teaspoon ground cinnamon
1 teaspoon salt
1/4 teaspoon baking soda
2 tablespoons grated orange peel

1 teaspoon vanilla extract
1 egg, lightly beaten
2 cups whole wheat pastry flour

Makes 1 loaf; 20 slices
Each slice contains approximately:
.8 gram of fiber
75 calories

In a mixing bowl soften yeast in the warmed orange juice. Warm the cottage cheese in the saucepan and combine with yeast mixture. Add all remaining ingredients except flour and mix well. Then add the flour, a little at a time, mixing well. Cover with a tea towel and allow to stand at room temperature for several hours or until doubled in bulk. Stir dough until again reduced to original size, and put it in a well-greased, standard-sized loaf pan. Cover the loaf pan and allow the dough to again double in bulk. Bake in a preheated 350° oven for 40 minutes.

This bread is delicious right from the oven. However, it's much easier to slice when cool. Wrap sliced bread in foil and store in the refrigerator until ready to use.

Serving Suggestions
Slice the bread and spread each slice with butter or margarine. Put the loaf back together again, wrap it tightly in foil and heat it in a preheated 350° oven for 20 minutes.

Slice the bread and spread each slice lightly with butter or margarine and place the slices under the broiler until lightly toasted. This is the way I like it best!

ROUGHAGE ROLLS

1-1/2 tablespoons active dry yeast (2 packages)
2 tablespoons date "sugar"
1 cup milk, warmed
1/2 teaspoon salt
1 egg, lightly beaten
3 to 3-1/2 cups whole wheat pastry flour
1/4 pound butter or corn oil margarine, melted
2 tablespoons grated Parmesan cheese

2 tablespoons unprocessed wheat bran
1 tablespoon hulled sesame seeds
1 teaspoon garlic salt

Makes 36 rolls
Each roll contains approximately:
.3 gram of fiber
50 calories

Combine yeast, date "sugar" and 1/4 cup of the warm milk. Set aside, out of a draft, and allow to double in bulk. This only takes a few minutes.

While the yeast is rising, combine the remaining 3/4 cup warm milk, salt and egg and mix well. Combine the milk-egg mixture with the yeast mixture in a large bowl. Add the flour 1 cup at a time, mixing thoroughly. Work the last 1/2 cup of flour in by kneading with your hands until the dough is smooth and elastic, about 10 minutes. Cover and allow to double in bulk, about 1-1/2 hours.

Punch down to original size. Pinch off walnut-sized balls of dough, dipping each ball in the melted butter or margarine. Place the dough balls in an ungreased baking dish. Mix the cheese, bran, sesame seeds and garlic salt together in a bowl. Sprinkle the mixture evenly over all of the rolls. Pour any remaining butter or margarine over the rolls. Place the rolls, covered, in a warm place and allow to double in size, about 30 minutes. Bake in a preheated 325° oven for 25 to 30 minutes, or until top sounds hollow when tapped. Remove from the oven and serve warm.

WHOLE WHEAT POPOVERS

1 cup whole wheat pastry flour
1/2 teaspoon salt
3 eggs, beaten
1 cup milk
2 tablespoons butter or corn oil margarine,
  melted

Makes 12 popovers
Each popover contains approximately:
.2 gram of fiber
85 calories

Preheat the oven to 450°. Grease muffin tins (preferably cast iron or Teflon), and place tins in the oven to heat.

Combine flour and salt and mix well. Combine beaten eggs and milk and mix well. Add the milk and egg mixture to the flour and mix well. Add the melted butter or margarine and mix well—but do not overmix!

Fill each of the heated muffin tins one-third full with the popover batter. Bake at 450° for 20 minutes. Reduce heat to 350° and bake for about 10 to 15 minutes longer. Do not open the oven door until after 30 minutes baking time, or the popovers may fall.

Serve immediately. I like to serve these popovers with butter or margarine and Berry-Bran Jam for breakfast.

Variations For appetizers or desserts, use a smaller-holed tin and fill the popovers with seafood or other savory filling, or flavored custard, whipped cream or ice cream.

CURRIED CORN MUFFINS

1/4 cup date "sugar"
1/2 cup low-fat milk
1/2 cup yellow cornmeal
1-1/2 cups whole wheat pastry flour
4 teaspoons baking powder
1 teaspoon salt
1 teaspoon curry powder
1 egg, beaten

1 teaspoon vanilla extract
1/4 cup corn oil
1 cup cooked corn kernels

Makes 12 muffins
Each muffin contains approximately:
.7 gram of fiber
150 calories

breads, pasta, pancakes, cereals

Preheat the oven to 400°. Combine date "sugar" and milk and allow to stand for 10 minutes. Combine cornmeal, flour, baking powder, salt and curry powder in a large mixing bowl and mix well. Combine the beaten egg, vanilla extract, corn oil and corn in another bowl and mix well.

Pour the liquid ingredients into the dry ingredients, add the date "sugar" and milk and stir until mixed but still lumpy.

Fill 12 2-1/2-inch muffin tins two-thirds full. Bake in the preheated oven for 25 minutes. Serve hot and enjoy the compliments!

BANANA MUFFINS

1 cup date "sugar"
4 tablespoons butter or corn oil margarine, at room temperature
2 eggs, lightly beaten
2 large ripe bananas, mashed
1 cup plus 2 tablespoons whole wheat pastry flour

1/2 teaspoon salt
1 teaspoon baking soda

Makes 14 2-1/2-inch muffins
Each muffin contains approximately:
.9 gram of fiber
150 calories

Preheat the oven to 325°. Cream the date "sugar" and butter or margarine together until smooth. In a small mixing bowl combine the beaten eggs and mashed bananas and mix well. Then add them to the date "sugar" mixture and again mix well. Set aside for 10 minutes.

In a mixing bowl, combine the flour, salt and baking soda. Add the flour to the wet ingredients, being careful not to overmix.

Divide the batter into greased muffin tins, or put paper baking cups in the muffin tins. Do not fill them over two-thirds full. Bake in the preheated oven for about 30 to 40 minutes. Allow muffins to cool for 10 minutes before removing papers.

I always use paper baking cups to make my Banana Muffins for two reasons: the muffin tin is easier to wash and the muffins freeze beautifully in the paper cups. Mildred Mead says that Banana Muffins are the only bread she likes with curry. Try it—I think you will agree!

breads, pasta, pancakes, cereals

TOASTED TORTILLA TRIANGLES

12 corn tortillas
salt

Makes 72 triangles
6 triangles contain approximately:
.3 gram of fiber
60 calories

Preheat the oven to 400°. Cut each tortilla into 6 pie-shaped pieces. Spread out half the tortilla triangles on a cookie sheet and salt lightly. Bake them in a preheated oven for 10 minutes. Remove from oven, turn each one over and return them to the oven for 3 more minutes. Remove from sheet and set aside. Place the remaining tortilla triangles on the cookie sheet and repeat process.

Toasted Tortilla Triangles are marvelous to serve with dips, with salads and soups, or crumbled up in casserole dishes. I like to serve them with my Gazpacho.

If you prefer smaller chips, cut the tortillas into smaller triangles before toasting them. They are so much fresher tasting than the tortilla chips you buy at the store and more importantly they are fat-free and lower in calories.

Variations Sprinkle the tortillas with seasoned salts, ground cumin or chili powder for different flavors.

BREAD CROUTONS AND BREAD CRUMBS

4 slices dry whole wheat bread

Makes 2 cups
1/2 cup contains approximately:
.4 gram of fiber
70 calories

If you do not have dry bread, separate slices of fresh bread and leave them on a countertop for several hours, turning occasionally, until they can be cut up easily. Slice the bread in 1/4-inch squares. Place squares in a large shallow pan or on a cookie sheet, and put in a 300° oven for 20 minutes or until a golden brown. Turn a few times so squares will brown evenly.

If you desire to make bread crumbs, you may either dry the bread 1 or 2 days until it is hard, or break it up into pieces and put it in the blender to make bread crumbs. If you wish toasted bread crumbs, put the toasted croutons in the blender.

PUMPERNICKEL CRISPS

1 loaf unsliced pumpernickel bread, frozen
2 garlic buds, crushed
1/2 cup grated Romano cheese
1/4 pound butter or corn oil margarine,
    melted

Makes about 35 slices
2 slices contain approximately:
.4 gram of fiber
140 calories

Preheat the oven to 300°. Using a sharp knife slice the frozen bread paper thin. Arrange slices on an ungreased baking sheet. Add remaining ingredients to the melted butter or margarine and using a pastry brush, spread the mixture evenly over the pumpernickel slices. Bake in a preheated oven for 15 to 20 minutes. Each slice should curl slightly on the edges. Cool to room temperature and store in an airtight container.

    Pumpernickel Crisps make excellent hors d'oeuvre and are good with soups and salads.

CHEESE STRAWS

1 cup whole wheat pastry flour
1 teaspoon baking powder
1/4 teaspoon salt
2 tablespoons butter or corn oil margarine
1 cup grated sharp cheddar cheese
1/3 cup ice water

paprika or cayenne pepper

Makes 70 Cheese Straws
Each straw contains approximately:
trace of fiber
12 calories

Preheat the oven to 425°. Combine flour, baking powder and salt in a mixing bowl. Add butter or margarine and blend well using a pastry blender. Add cheese and continue mixing with the pastry blender until the dough looks like coarse cornmeal. Add ice water and mix well.

    Put the dough on a floured board and roll out about 1/8 inch thick. Fold the edges over so that all edges are straight and press them down. Sprinkle paprika or cayenne pepper lightly over the dough. Cut into 1/4-inch-wide strips about 3 inches long.

    Place the strips on a lightly greased cookie sheet and bake 8 to 10 minutes in the center of the preheated oven. If not crisp enough reduce oven temperature to 350° and cook for 5 more minutes or until crisp. Cool the straws before removing them from the cookie sheet.

    Cheese Straws are good for snacks and hors d'oeuvre.. They are also good served with soups and salads. Store in a covered container. To re-crisp, put them in a 350° oven for 10 minutes.

breads, pasta, pancakes, cereals

WHOLE WHEAT SOFT PRETZELS

1 scant tablespoon active dry yeast (1 package)
1 teaspoon date "sugar"
1-1/4 cups warm water
3 to 3-1/2 cups whole wheat flour
2 teaspoons salt
butter or corn oil margarine
4 teaspoons baking soda

kosher salt

Makes 24 pretzels
Each pretzel contains approximately:
.5 gram of fiber
70 calories

Dissolve the yeast and date "sugar" in 1/4 cup of the warm water and allow to double in bulk. This only takes a few minutes. Combine the flour and salt in a large mixing bowl. Add the remaining 1 cup of water and the yeast mixture and mix well. Add enough additional flour to make a stiff dough if necessary.

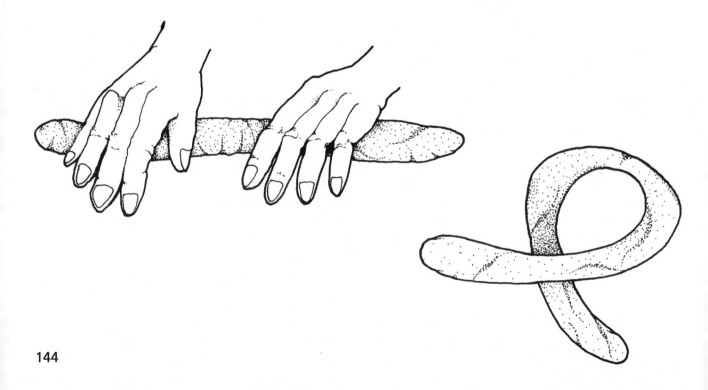

Knead the dough until it is shiny and feels elastic, about 10 minutes. Form the dough into a ball and coat with butter or corn oil margarine. Place the ball of dough in a bowl and cover with a towel. Allow dough to rise until double in bulk, about 1-1/2 hours.

Divide the dough into 12 pieces. Roll each piece with your hands to form a rope approximately 20 inches long and 1/4 inch in diameter. Shape each rope into a pretzel shape. Wet your fingers to pinch the pretzel together firmly.

Put 4 cups of water in a large pan, add the baking soda and bring to a boil. Carefully lower each pretzel into the boiling water and boil approximately 1 minute or until the pretzel floats to the top. Remove the pretzel from the water with a slotted spatula and place on a plate to drain.

After all of the water has drained off the pretzel, carefully place the pretzel on a greased baking sheet. Sprinkle the pretzel with kosher salt.

Bake in a preheated 350° oven for approximately 25 minutes or until a golden brown. Serve warm or reheat before serving. These pretzels are much better when served warm.

breads, pasta, pancakes, cereals

WHEAT GERM WAFFLES

1 cup non-fat milk
2 tablespoons date "sugar"
4 eggs, separated
1/4 teaspoon salt
1 cup water
2 tablespoons corn oil
2 cups whole wheat flour

1 cup wheat germ

Makes 6 servings
Each serving contains approximately:
1.6 grams of fiber
290 calories

Combine milk and date "sugar" and set aside for at least 10 minutes. Beat the egg whites until stiff but not dry and set aside.

Beat the yolks with a fork. Add the date "sugar" and milk, salt, water and corn oil and mix well. Combine the flour and wheat germ in a large mixing bowl. Add the milk mixture and mix thoroughly. Fold in the beaten egg whites. Cook in a preheated waffle iron until well browned and crisp.

I love Wheat Germ Waffles served with Date Butter and toasted nuts or seeds.

SUPER BAKED PANCAKE

1/2 cup low-fat milk, at room temperature
1 teaspoon date "sugar"
1/4 teaspoon salt
1/8 teaspoon ground nutmeg
2 eggs, lightly beaten and at room temperature
1/4 teaspoon vanilla extract

2 tablespoons butter or corn oil margarine

Makes 4 servings
Each serving contains approximately:
.4 gram of fiber
170 calories

Preheat the oven to 400°. Combine the milk and date "sugar" and set aside for 10 minutes. Then combine all the ingredients except butter or margarine in a mixing bowl. Beat lightly leaving the batter a little lumpy. Melt the butter or margarine in a 10-inch iron skillet. When it starts to bubble and the skillet is hot, pour the batter into the skillet and bake in the preheated oven for about 20 minutes or until the pancake is golden brown.

Remove the pancake from the oven and cut it into 4 pie-shaped pieces or bring the skillet to the table to show your guests how pretty it looks before you cut it. I like it best served with Sherried Fruit Topping spooned on the top of the whole pancake while it is still in the skillet. I bring the skillet to the table and then cut the pancake and serve it, spooning sour cream on the top of each fruit-topped "piece of pancake." Super Baked Pancake is also delicious sprinkled with date "sugar" and fresh lemon juice or spread with Date Butter.

GINGERBREAD PANCAKES

1 cup strong brewed coffee (or use 2 teaspoons instant decaffeinated coffee and 1 cup hot water)
3/4 cup date "sugar"
1 cup whole wheat flour
3/4 teaspoon baking soda
1/2 teaspoon ground ginger
1/2 teaspoon ground cinnamon
1/4 teaspoon salt

1/4 teaspoon ground cloves
1 egg, beaten
4 tablespoons butter or corn oil margarine, melted

Makes 12 small pancakes
Each pancake contains approximately:
.7 gram of fiber
125 calories

Combine coffee and date "sugar" and allow to stand for 10 minutes. Combine flour, baking soda, ginger, cinnamon, salt and cloves in a large mixing bowl. In another bowl, combine the beaten egg, melted butter or margarine and coffee-date "sugar" mixture.

Add the liquid ingredients to the dry ingredients and mix just enough to moisten all dry ingredients. Batter should remain lumpy. Drop by spoonfuls onto a hot greased griddle or skillet. Cook until the top of each pancake is covered with tiny bubbles and the bubbles begin to break, making little holes all over the top of the pancake. Turn pancakes and brown on the other side.

I like Gingerbread Pancakes best spread lightly with Date Butter and a spoonful of sour cream on top. I have even heard of people who serve them with whipped cream! Cook all the batter and save leftover pancakes for snacks and school lunches.

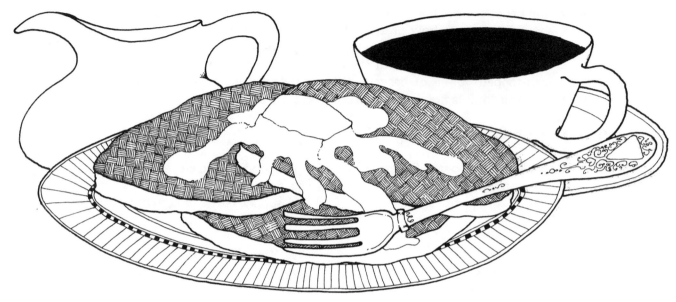

GERMAN PANCAKES

2 eggs
1/4 teaspoon baking soda
1/4 teaspoon salt
1/8 teaspoon dry mustard
2-1/2 teaspoons baking powder
1 cup buttermilk
1 cup whole wheat flour

1 teaspoon butter or corn oil margarine
Date Butter, page 49

Makes 14 4-inch pancakes
Each pancake contains approximately:
.2 gram of fiber
50 calories

Beat the eggs, baking soda, salt, mustard and baking powder together until frothy. Add the buttermilk and whole wheat flour. Mix well. Heat a cured iron skillet or Teflon pan. Add butter and allow it to melt as the pan heats. When the pan is hot, wipe the butter out with a paper towel. Using a soup ladle, pour out the batter and cook the pancakes over moderate heat.

Cook until the top of each pancake is covered with tiny bubbles and the bubbles begin to break, making little holes all over the top of the pancake. Turn pancakes and brown on them on the other side.

Spread each pancake lightly with Date Butter. Serve German Pancakes with applesauce and sausage for a truly hearty German breakfast.

BUCKWHEAT BLINI

2 cups buckwheat flour
2 teaspoons baking powder
3/4 teaspoon salt
1/2 teaspoon baking soda
1 egg, beaten
2 cups low-fat milk
1 tablespoon butter or corn oil margarine,
   melted

2 teaspoons butter or corn oil margarine

Makes 48 blini
3 blini contain approximately:
.2 gram of fiber
75 calories

In a large mixing bowl combine the buckwheat flour, baking powder, salt and baking soda. In another bowl combine the beaten egg and milk and mix well. Slowly add the liquid to the dry ingredients, stirring to form a smooth batter. Add the melted butter or margarine and mix well.

Heat a cured iron skillet or Teflon pan. Add the remaining butter or corn oil margarine and allow it to melt as the pan heats. When the pan is hot, wipe the butter or margarine out using a paper towel. Use a large spoon or soup ladle to pour out the batter into the pan. Each blini should be approximately 3 inches in diameter. Cook the blini over moderate heat until brown on both sides.

I love Buckwheat Blini with sour cream and caviar either for an hors d'oeuvre or an unusual entrée. When serving Blini au Caviar for lunch, I start with a Watercress Salad and serve fresh fruit for dessert.

POWERFUL PORRIDGE

1 cup unprocessed wheat bran
2 cups rolled oats
1/2 cup chopped almonds
1 cup chopped dried prunes
1/2 cup raisins
1 teaspoon ground cinnamon

4 cups water

Makes 6 cups
1/2 cup contains approximately:
1.4 grams of fiber
179 calories

Combine all dry ingredients in a mixing bowl and mix well. Add the water, mix well, cover and refrigerate overnight before serving. It is even better to wait 2 or 3 days before serving.

Serve Powerful Porridge cold. I like it best plain or with a few slices of banana on top. My family likes it better with milk or yogurt on it. It is also good with ricotta or cottage cheese.   149

GREAT GRANOLA

1/4 cup sesame oil
1/2 teaspoon salt
1 teaspoon vanilla extract
3-1/2 cups rolled oats
1/2 cup unprocessed wheat bran
1/2 cup chopped almonds
1/2 cup sunflower seeds

1 cup date "sugar"
1/2 cup raisins

Makes 4 cups
1/4 cup contains approximately:
1.2 grams of fiber
200 calories

Preheat the oven to 325°. Combine sesame oil, salt and vanilla and mix thoroughly. Add all other ingredients, except date "sugar" and raisins, and mix well.

Spread the mixture evenly on a cookie sheet with sides and bake in the preheated oven for 15 minutes. Remove from the oven and add date "sugar." Stir well and continue baking for another 10 to 15 minutes or until lightly browned. Stir occasionally while cooking to brown evenly. Remove from the oven and immediately mix with the raisins. Cool to room temperature and store in a tightly covered container.

CRUNCHY CAROB GRANOLA

1/2 cup sesame oil
1 teaspoon vanilla extract
1/2 teaspoon salt
3-1/2 cups rolled oats
1/2 cup unprocessed wheat bran
1 cup chopped raw cashews
3/4 cup date "sugar"

1 cup carob chips

Makes 4 cups
1/4 cup contains approximately:
.6 gram of fiber
220 calories

Preheat the oven to 325°. Combine sesame oil, vanilla and salt and mix thoroughly. Add all other ingredients except the date "sugar" and carob chips and mix well.

Spread the mixture evenly on a cookie sheet with sides and bake in the preheated oven for 15 minutes. Remove from the oven and add the date "sugar." Stir well and continue baking for another 10 to 15 minutes or until lightly browned. Stir occasionally while cooking to brown evenly. Remove from the oven and immediately mix with the carob chips. Cool to room temperature and store in a tightly covered container.

FIBER FETTUCCINI PASTA

2 cups whole wheat pastry flour
1/4 cup unprocessed wheat bran
2 tablespoons olive oil
3/4 cup warm water

Makes 4 cups cooked noodles
1/2 cup contains approximately:
1.0 gram of fiber
140 calories

Using a pastry blender, combine the flour, bran and oil, cutting through it evenly until well mixed. Add water, a little at a time, to form a firm ball of dough. This process is best done by kneading by hand until dough becomes shiny, smooth and elastic. Cover the ball with an inverted bowl and allow to stand at room temperature for at least 1 hour. Then divide the ball of dough into 4 equal parts. Flatten each piece with the palm of your hand into a square-shaped section about 1 inch thick. With a heavy rolling pin on a lightly floured board, roll out dough lengthwise, turn, and roll out crosswise. Continue with this until you have pasta to desired thickness, about 1/8 inch thick or less. Do this with each divided section of dough. To prevent sticking while rolling out the dough, carefully lift it and sprinkle a little more flour on the board.

For fettuccini, cut this into 1/4-inch-wide strips. For lasagne, cut into 2-1/2-inch-wide strips.

To Cook Pasta
Use a large kettle (6-quart) filled with water, adding 2 tablespoons of salt and 1 tablespoon of olive oil. Bring the water to a boil and add the pasta. Boil for approximately 7 to 8 minutes or to taste. Pasta made with bran will take a couple of minutes longer to cook than regular pasta. When cooked it should be what the Italians call al dente, meaning it is slightly firm to the bite. Pour the water and pasta into a colander and drain well. The fettuccini is now ready to be mixed with your favorite sauce. My favorite recipes for Fiber Fettuccini are Fettuccini al Jeanno and Fettuccini Florentine.

FETTUCCINI AL JEANNO

4 cups cooked Fiber Fettuccini Pasta, preceding
4 tablespoons butter or margarine
1/4 teaspoon garlic powder
1/2 cup freshly grated Romano cheese
1/4 teaspoon freshly ground black pepper

Makes 8 servings
Each serving contains approximately:
1.0 gram of fiber
200 calories

While the fettuccini is cooking, melt the butter or margarine and add the garlic powder, mixing thoroughly. When the pasta is ready, pour it into a colander or large strainer and drain well. Pour the pasta into a bowl, pour the garlic butter over it and mix thoroughly. Add the Romano cheese and pepper and again mix well. Serve at once.

I like to serve this with Pizza Chicken and a large tossed green salad with Italian Fiber Dressing. This is my higher fiber version of the famous Fettuccini Alfredo served in Rome.

WHOLE WHEAT NOODLES

2 cups whole wheat flour
1-1/2 tablespoons corn oil
3/4 cup warm water

Makes 4 cups cooked noodles
1/2 cup contains approximately:
.7 gram of fiber
120 calories

Using a pastry blender, combine the flour and corn oil, cutting through it evenly until well mixed. Add water, a little at a time, to form a firm ball of dough. This process is best done by kneading by hand until dough becomes shiny, smooth and elastic. Cover the ball with an inverted bowl and allow to stand at room temperature for at least 1 hour. Then divide the ball of dough into 4 equal parts. Flatten each piece with the palm of your hand into a square-shaped section about 1 inch thick. With a heavy rolling pin on a lightly floured board, roll out dough lengthwise, turn, and roll out crosswise. Continue with this until you have noodles to desired thickness, about 1/8 inch thick or less. Do this with each divided section of dough. To prevent sticking while rolling out the dough, carefully lift it and sprinkle a little more flour on the board. Cut rolled-out dough into 1-inch-wide strips.

To Cook Noodles

Use a large kettle (6-quart) filled with water, adding 2 tablespoons of salt and 1 tablespoon of corn oil. Bring the water to a boil and add the noodles. Boil for approximately 8 to 10 minutes or to taste. Pour the water and noodles into a colander and drain well. The noodles are now ready to be eaten as they are or mixed with your favorite sauce. I like them with Dave's Hash.

sweets and desserts

This section is designed to satisfy your sweet tooth, keep your dentist happy with all of your teeth and delight your family and friends with your delicious desserts.

For those of you who share my love for pies *and* my dislike for making pie crusts because of the mess it makes, try making my Perfect Pie Crusts. They will open up a whole new world of pie baking for you.

My favorite recipe in this section is Fabulous Fruit Cake. I make it for everybody's birthday, serve it during the holidays and if there is any left over, serve it for breakfast the next morning as coffee cake.

BRAN-MANGO MOUSSE
("The Dynamic Duo")

1 cup Jelled Milk, page 47
1/2 cup low-fat milk
1 large ripe mango, peeled and chopped
   (1-1/2 cups)
2 tablespoons unprocessed wheat bran
1 tablespoon date "sugar"
1/2 teaspoon vanilla extract

Makes 6 servings
Each serving contains approximately:
.4 gram of fiber
53 calories

Put all ingredients in a blender and blend on high speed until very frothy. Pour into 6 sherbet glasses and chill until set. (Instead of putting all the mango in the blender, you may want to put part of the diced mango in the bottom of each sherbet glass or bowl and pour the whipped mixture over it.)

The ranking order of fruits and vegetables in terms of their water-holding and swelling ability lists bran number one and mango number two. This water-holding characteristic is considered beneficial, so I subtitled my favorite mousse "the dynamic duo"! This is not only a delicious and unusual dessert, but it is also good for you!

sweets and desserts

FABULOUS FRUIT CAKE

1/2 cup finely chopped almonds
1/2 cup sunflower seeds
2 cups whole wheat flour
1 teaspoon salt
1-1/2 cups rolled oats
1/2 cup unprocessed wheat bran
1 cup sesame oil
2 teaspoons vanilla extract
1 egg, lightly beaten
3 cups crushed fresh pineapple or canned
   in natural juice
1 cup unsweetened shredded coconut
1 cup raisins
1-1/2 cups Fabulous Frosting, following

Makes 14 servings as a two-layer cake
Each serving contains approximately:
1.9 grams of fiber
472 calories

Makes 24 servings as two one-layer cakes
Each serving contains approximately:
1.1 grams of fiber
275 calories

Preheat the oven to 350°. Place the chopped almonds and sunflower seeds on a cookie sheet in the preheated oven for approximately 10 minutes or until a golden brown. Watch carefully as they burn easily. Set aside.

Combine flour, salt, rolled oats and bran in a large mixing bowl and mix well. Add oil, vanilla extract and egg to the dry ingredients and mix well. Add all other ingredients, except the Fabulous Frosting, and mix thoroughly, forming a soft crumbly dough. Divide the dough in half and place each half in a well-greased, 9-inch cake pan. Press the dough down firmly. Bake in a 350° oven for 40 to 50 minutes. Allow to cool in the pans on a rack for 15 minutes before turning out the cakes onto plates. Cool to room temperature.

Spread half of the Fabulous Frosting on the top of each cake. Set one cake on top of the other to make a two-layer cake, or serve as two one-layer cakes for more servings and fewer calories per serving. The smaller serving is as large as most people want because it is very rich.

This makes a *fabulous* birthday cake for the people you really love and want to be super-healthy.

FABULOUS FROSTING

1 cup date "sugar"
3/4 cup water
1/4 cup (2 ounces) cream cheese, at room
   temperature
4 tablespoons butter or corn oil margarine
1 teaspoon vanilla extract

1/4 teaspoon ground cinnamon

Makes 1-1/2 cups
1 tablespoon contains approximately:
.3 gram of fiber
60 calories

Combine date "sugar" and water in a saucepan. Bring to a boil over medium heat. Reduce heat and simmer, uncovered, for 20 to 25 minutes or until all water is absorbed. Remove from heat and cool to room temperature. Combine all ingredients in a bowl and using a pastry blender, mix until a smooth consistency.

Fabulous Frosting is delicious on cakes and cookies. It is also a fabulous pancake and waffle topping. I even like it on toast, English muffins, bagels, etc.

BROILED BANANAS

3 large, not too ripe, bananas
2 tablespoons butter or corn oil margarine,
   melted
2 tablespoons date "sugar"

Makes 6 servings
Each serving contains approximately:
.6 gram of fiber
118 calories

Peel the bananas and slice in half lengthwise. Put the banana halves, cut side up, in a large baking dish or on a cookie sheet. Brush the melted butter or margarine over them using a pastry brush. Then sprinkle the date "sugar" evenly over each banana half. Place the bananas under the broiler until the date "sugar" has turned a deep rich brown (not black). You must watch them carefully because the date "sugar" browns quickly.

Broiled Bananas are delicious and versatile. I always serve them with Green Eggs and Ham en Croustade for brunch. They are also a wonderful light dessert after a heavy meal.

sweets and desserts

BRAN-BAKED APPLESAUCE

3 large green cooking apples
1 cup water
1/4 cup date "sugar"
4 teaspoons unprocessed wheat bran
1/2 teaspoon ground cinnamon
1/4 teaspoon ground nutmeg

1/2 teaspoon vanilla extract

Makes 2 cups
1/2 cup contains approximately:
2.1 grams of fiber
125 calories

Preheat oven to 325°. Dice apples into 1-inch cubes, removing the core completely. Mix all other ingredients in the water. Place the diced apples in a glass loaf pan or baking dish. (I prefer a loaf pan because the apples stay moister.) Pour the water mixture over the apples. Bake, uncovered, in the preheated oven for 45 minutes. Remove from oven and allow baked apples to come to room temperature. Store in the refrigerator.

This applesauce is an excellent accompaniment to many meats. It's a good breakfast fruit, a light dessert and the basic ingredient for Applesauce Topping.

If you prefer a smooth, creamy applesauce, put the baked apples and all the cooking liquid in a blender and blend until smooth. If necessary, add 1/4 cup more water to make a creamier consistency.

APPLESAUCE TOPPING

2 cups Bran-Baked Applesauce, preceding
1/4 cup water
1/4 teaspoon ground cinnamon
1 teaspoon vanilla extract
1 tablespoon date "sugar"

Makes 2 cups
1/2 cup contains approximately:
2.3 grams of fiber
146 calories

Place all ingredients in blender and blend until smooth. This is a marvelous sauce with a wide variety of uses. It is fabulous over German Pancakes. It is also good on French toast and blintzes.

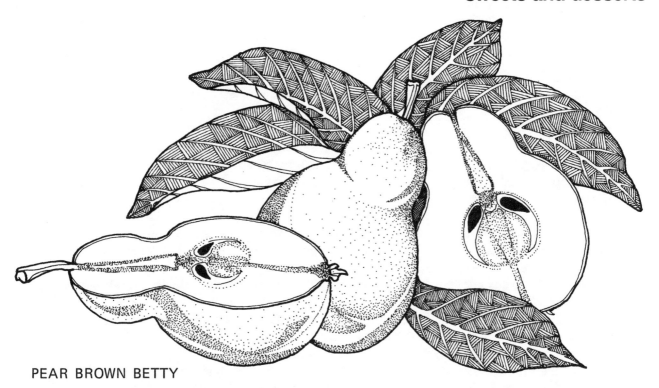

PEAR BROWN BETTY

1/4 pound butter or corn oil margarine,
   melted
3/4 cup date "sugar"
4 cups soft, whole wheat bread crumbs,
   loosely packed
4 very ripe pears, cored and thinly sliced
   (5 cups sliced)
2 tablespoons unprocessed wheat bran

1/2 teaspoon salt
1/2 teaspoon ground ginger
1/2 teaspoon ground cinnamon

Makes 12 servings
Each serving contains approximately:
1.9 grams of fiber
292 calories

Preheat oven to 375°. Combine melted butter or margarine and date "sugar" and allow to stand 10 minutes. Combine bread crumbs with butter and date "sugar" mixture and toss until well mixed. Combine sliced pears and all other ingredients and mix well. Place one-half of the bread crumbs in a greased 2-quart casserole. Spoon the pear mixture evenly over the bread crumbs. Top with remaining bread crumbs. Cover and bake in the preheated oven for 30 minutes. Uncover and bake for 10 to 15 more minutes.

159

GARBANZO BEAN CAKE

1/4 pound dried garbanzo beans (1/2 cup)
1/2 cup low-fat milk
1/3 cup date "sugar"
corn oil margarine
3 eggs, separated
1/8 teaspoon salt
1/8 teaspoon ground nutmeg
1/4 teaspoon ground cinnamon

1/2 teaspoon vanilla extract
1 teaspoon rum extract

Makes 6 servings
Each serving contains approximately:
1.4 grams of fiber
153 calories

Wash the garbanzo beans thoroughly and put in a saucepan with a lid. Add enough water to cover the beans by about 2 inches. Bring to a boil, reduce heat and simmer 2-1/2 hours or until tender. Drain and let cool.

While the beans are cooking combine the milk and date "sugar." Cover and refrigerate until ready to use.

Preheat the oven to 350°. Lightly grease the sides of a 9-inch cake pan with corn oil margarine. Cut wax paper to fit the bottom of the pan. (If you are using a Teflon pan, put the wax paper on the bottom, but it is not necessary to grease the sides.)

Put the drained garbanzo beans, milk and date "sugar" in a blender and blend until smooth. Allow to stand for 10 minutes. Beat the egg whites and salt until stiff but not dry and set aside. (Always beat the egg whites before the yolks because then you don't have to wash the beater in between. Egg whites must be beaten with a very clean, dry beater!) Beat the egg yolks until thick. Add all other ingredients, except beaten whites, to the beaten yolks and mix thoroughly. Fold in the egg whites.

Pour the batter into the cake pan and bake in the preheated oven for approximately 40 minutes or until the cake is firm in the center. Cool the cake on a rack for 10 minutes, then remove the cake from the pan and carefully peel off the wax paper. Cool to room temperature, then cover and refrigerate several hours or overnight before serving.

I personally like fresh pineapple with this cake, however, any fresh fruit in season would be good and make a colorful and unusual dessert course.

RR DESSERT
(Raid Refrigerator)

2 cups Powerful Porridge, page 149
1 cup Date-Cheese Dressing, page 62
4 whole almonds for garnish (optional)

Makes 4 servings
Each serving contains approximately:
2.3 grams of fiber
305 calories

Using 4 sherbet glasses, put a 1/2-cup round scoop of Powerful Porridge in each glass. Spoon 1/4 cup of Date-Cheese Dressing on the top of each serving. Garnish each serving with 1 whole almond.

I discovered this combination one day when my husband asked me what new creation we were having for dessert. I didn't have anything prepared so I just combined what I had in the refrigerator. He said, "This is delicious and so different. Is it some new kind of ice cream?" I didn't tell him what it was. I was afraid he would lose his enthusiasm if he knew he was eating last night's fruit salad dressing on this morning's breakfast cereal!

GOLDEN RICE PUDDING

2 cups cooked brown rice
2 tablespoons unprocessed wheat bran
2 cups low-fat milk
4 eggs, beaten
1/4 cup date "sugar"
1 tablespoon ground cinnamon
2 teaspoons vanilla extract

1 cup raisins

Makes 8 servings
Each serving contains approximately:
.7 gram of fiber
195 calories

Preheat oven to 350°. Combine all ingredients in a large mixing bowl and mix well. Pour into a greased 2-quart casserole and set the casserole in a metal pan filled with hot water to a depth of 3/4 inch. Bake in the preheated oven for 1 hour and 15 minutes.

This is good served hot as an unusual brunch entrée. When using it for brunch I serve it with Canadian bacon or ham slices. It is also a good dessert, hot or cold. If you plan to serve it cold, cool to room temperature and then refrigerate until cold.

sweets and desserts

PERFECT PIE CRUST

1 cup whole wheat pastry flour
1/4 teaspoon salt
1/4 cup corn oil
3 tablespoons ice water

Makes 1 9-inch pie crust
1 pie crust contains approximately:
2.8 grams of fiber
940 calories

Preheat the oven to 375°. Put flour and salt in a 9-inch pie pan and mix well. Measure the oil in a large measuring cup. Add the water to the oil and mix well, using a fork.

Slowly add the liquid to the flour mixture in the pie pan, mixing it with the same fork. Continue mixing until all ingredients are well blended. Press into shape with your fingers. Make sure that the crust covers the entire inner surface of the pie pan evenly. Prick the bottom of the crust with a fork in several places and place in a 375° oven for 20 to 25 minutes or until a golden brown if the recipe calls for a prebaked crust.

I used to hate making my own pie crust because I always messed up the entire kitchen and had flour all over me *and* the floor. Then one day when I was in a hurry I just put all of the ingredients in the pie pan, carefully mixed them together and then pressed the dough out with my fingers. It was so delicious *and* so easy that I have never gone back to rolling out dough on a floured board again. This recipe has actually made pie making fun for me. That is why it's called Perfect Pie Crust!

PERFECT BRAN PIE CRUST

3/4 cup whole wheat pastry flour
1/4 cup unprocessed wheat bran
1/4 teaspoon salt
1/4 cup corn oil
3 tablespoons ice water

Makes 1 9-inch pie crust
1 pie crust contains approximately:
4.4 grams of fiber
893 calories

Preheat the oven to 375°. Put flour, bran and salt in a 9-inch pie pan and mix well. Measure the oil in a measuring cup. Add the water to the oil and mix well, using a fork.

Slowly add the liquid to the flour-bran mixture in the pie pan, mixing it with the same fork. Continue mixing until all ingredients are well blended. Press it into shape with your fingers, making sure it covers the entire inner surface of the pie pan evenly. Prick the bottom of the crust with a fork and place in a 375° oven for 20 minutes if the recipe you are using calls for a prebaked pie crust.

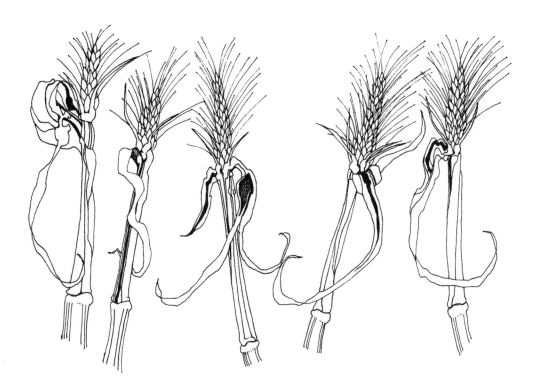

PERFECT GRAHAM-BRAN PIE CRUST

3/4 cup graham cracker crumbs
   (10-1/2 graham crackers)
1/4 cup unprocessed wheat bran
4 tablespoons butter or corn oil margarine
3 tablespoons date "sugar"

Makes 1 9-inch pie crust
1 pie crust contains approximately:
3.8 grams of fiber
1019 calories

Preheat the oven to 375°. Put graham cracker crumbs and bran in a 9-inch pie pan and mix well. Melt the butter or margarine, combine with the date "sugar" and allow to stand 10 minutes. Then add the butter mixture to the crumbs. Mix well, using a fork, until all ingredients are thoroughly blended. Press into shape with your fingers, making sure the crust covers the entire inner surface of the pie pan evenly. Prick the bottom of the crust with a fork in several places and place in the center of a 375° oven for 8 minutes if the recipe you are using calls for a prebaked pie crust.

sweets and desserts

STRAWBERRY CREAM PIE

1 prebaked Perfect Bran Pie Crust, page 162
1 scant tablespoon (1 envelope)
   unflavored gelatin
1/4 cup water
1-1/2 cups low-fat milk
2 eggs, beaten
1/4 teaspoon salt
1/2 cup date "sugar"

1-1/2 teaspoons vanilla extract
2-1/2 cups strawberries

Makes 8 servings
Each serving contains approximately:
1.4 grams of fiber
208 calories

Prepare the pie crust and set aside. Soften the gelatin in the water and set aside. Bring the milk to the boiling point in the top of a double boiler over simmering water. Beat the eggs with the salt. Slowly pour the hot milk into the egg mixture, stirring with a wire whisk. Add the date "sugar" and vanilla and mix well. Return the mixture to the double boiler top and place it over the simmering water until the custard coats a metal spoon. Remove from the heat. Add the softened gelatin to the hot custard, stirring until the gelatin is completely dissolved. Cool this mixture to room temperature.

Carefully wash strawberries and remove the stems. Put aside the 4 largest strawberries to decorate the finished pie. Slice all of the other strawberries. Put half of the sliced strawberries into the baked pie shell. Mash the remaining strawberries, add them to the custard and mix well. Spoon the custard over the sliced strawberries in the pie crust. Cut the 4 reserved strawberries in half lengthwise and space them evenly around the outside edge of the pie so that each piece of pie will have a strawberry garnish. Chill the pie for at least 3 hours before serving.

DESERT LEMON CHIFFON PIE

1 prebaked Perfect Graham-Bran Pie Crust,
   page 163
1-1/2 teaspoons unflavored gelatin
1/3 cup water
3 egg yolks
1 tablespoon finely grated lemon peel
1/4 cup fresh lemon juice
1/4 teaspoon salt

1/2 cup date "sugar"
4 egg whites, beaten stiff but not dry

Makes 8 servings
Each serving contains approximately:
.9 gram of fiber
204 calories

Prepare the pie crust and set aside. Soften the gelatin in the water and set aside. Put the egg yolks in the top of a double boiler and beat well. Stir in the grated lemon peel, lemon juice, salt and date "sugar." Cook over boiling water 2 minutes, stirring constantly. Continue to cook and stir until the gelatin is completely dissolved and mixture has thickened slightly, about 2 to 3 minutes. Remove from the heat and cool to room temperature. Fold the beaten egg whites into the lemon mixture and spoon into the baked crust. Refrigerate until firm.

When your friends ask you why your lemon pie is caramel colored, tell them it is a Desert Lemon Chiffon Pie. Sugarcane does not grow in the desert so the pie is made from brown date "sugar" which gives it the color *and* is better for them!

sweets and desserts

PLUM PUDDING PIE

1 Perfect Pie Crust, unbaked, page 162
2 tablespoons unprocessed wheat bran
1 cup whole bran cereal
1/2 cup date "sugar"
1/3 cup fresh orange juice
2 tablespoons butter or corn oil margarine,
  at room temperature
1 teaspoon ground cinnamon
1/2 teaspoon ground nutmeg
1/8 teaspoon ground allspice

1/8 teaspoon ground cloves
2 cups shredded, tart green apples
  (3 medium apples)
1 tablespoon fresh lemon juice
1 tablespoon chopped raisins

Makes 8 servings
Each serving contains approximately:
2.1 grams of fiber
261 calories

Prepare the pie crust and set aside. Preheat the oven to 325°. Add the bran to the bran cereal and date "sugar" in a mixing bowl. Add the orange juice and mix well. Allow to stand for 10 minutes. While this mixture is softening in the orange juice, combine the butter or margarine, cinnamon, nutmeg, allspice and ground cloves in a large mixing bowl. Mix well using a pastry blender. Add the orange juice mixture and continue to blend with the pastry blender until all ingredients are thoroughly mixed and the consistency of coarse cornmeal. Combine the shredded apples and lemon juice and mix well. Add the shredded apple mixture and chopped raisins to the other ingredients and mix thoroughly. Spoon the plum pudding into the unbaked Perfect Pie

Crust and press it down firmly. Place the pie in the center of the preheated oven for 1 hour. Remove from the oven and cool the pie on a rack. Cool for at least 20 minutes before serving.

This is a "fabulously fibrous" dessert for a holiday feast (or any other time!). I always serve it with Rum Sauce.

RUM SAUCE

2 tablespoons cornstarch
2 cups water
1 cup date "sugar"
1/4 teaspoon salt
2 tablespoons butter or corn oil margarine
1 teaspoon vanilla extract

2 tablespoons dark rum

Makes 2 cups
1/4 cup contains approximately:
.9 gram of fiber
151 calories

In the top of a double boiler dissolve the cornstarch in 1/2 cup of the water. Add the remaining 1-1/2 cups of water and mix thoroughly. Add all other ingredients, except the rum, and put the top of the double boiler over boiling water. Bring to a boil and continue cooking, stirring frequently, until the sauce thickens, about 10 minutes. Lift the top of the double boiler off of the bottom and allow to cool for 5 minutes before adding the rum.

Serve warm over Plum Pudding Pie, cake or ice cream.

Brandy Sauce Variation Substitute 2 tablespoons brandy for the 2 tablespoons dark rum.

sweets and desserts

MY GRANDMOTHER'S PEACH COBBLER
(Well, almost!)

2-1/4 cups whole wheat pastry flour
1/4 cup unprocessed wheat bran
1/2 teaspoon baking powder
1/4 teaspoon baking soda
1/2 teaspoon salt
1/2 teaspoon ground cinnamon
1/4 pound butter or corn oil margarine,
   at room temperature
1 cup buttermilk
4 pounds peaches, peeled and sliced
   (about 8 cups sliced)

2 tablespoons ground cinnamon
1 cup date "sugar"
1-1/2 cups water
cinnamon for garnish

Makes 12 servings
Each serving contains approximately:
1.9 grams of fiber
274 calories

Preheat the oven to 350°. Put flour, bran, baking powder, baking soda, salt and 1/2 teaspoon cinnamon in a large mixing bowl and mix well. Add the butter or margarine and mix well, using a pastry blender. Add the buttermilk, a little at a time, until the dough is thoroughly mixed. Divide the dough into 2 balls. Put them on a lightly floured board and roll out each ball to a strip about 5 inches wide and 10 inches long.

Spread half of the peaches evenly over each strip of dough, leaving a narrow border. Sprinkle 1 tablespoon of cinnamon and 1/2 cup of date "sugar" evenly over the top of the peaches on each strip.

Roll each strip like a jelly roll, being careful not to spill the peach slices out of the roll. Put both rolls in a loaf pan or casserole and add the water. Sprinkle cinnamon lightly over the top. Bake, uncovered, in a 350° oven for 1 hour or until a golden brown on the top.

This is just like the peach cobbler my grandmother used to make with one exception: Her ingredients were a bit more refined because she wasn't really on to the need for dietary fiber in the daily diet. I recommend serving this cobbler warm with milk poured over the top, just the way my grandmother did!

FROZEN BONBONS

16 small (1-1/2-inch) Whole Wheat Popovers,
   page 139
1 cup Date "Sugar" Ice Milk, following
1 cup Crunchy Carob Sauce, page 170

Makes 8 servings
Each serving contains approximately:
1.0 gram of fiber
227 calories

Place the popovers on a cookie sheet and fill each one with 1 tablespoon Date "Sugar" Ice Milk. Then spoon 1 tablespoon Crunchy Carob Sauce over each puff. Put the cookie sheet in the freezer until the bonbons are frozen. Put each Frozen Bonbon in a small plastic bag and store in the freezer. Frozen Bonbons make a fabulous instant dessert and are also great to have on hand for snacks.

DATE "SUGAR" ICE MILK

1-1/2 teaspoons unflavored gelatin
2 tablespoons water
1 cup canned skim milk
1 tablespoon cornstarch
2 cups low-fat milk
2 teaspoons vanilla extract
3/4 cup date "sugar"
2 egg whites

dash salt
1/8 teaspoon cream of tartar

Makes 1 quart
1/2 cup contains approximately:
.7 gram of fiber
137 calories

Put the gelatin in the water and allow to soften. Pour 3/4 cup of the canned skim milk in the top of a double boiler. Add the cornstarch to the remaining 1/4 cup of canned milk and mix until thoroughly dissolved. Add the cornstarch mixture to the double boiler. Heat milk and cornstarch over simmering water until it comes to a boil, stirring constantly. Allow the mixture to simmer for about 3 minutes, or until slightly thickened.

    Remove from heat and add softened gelatin. Mix until all gelatin is completely dissolved. Add the low-fat milk, vanilla and date "sugar." Mix thoroughly. Place mixture in the refrigerator for at least 2 hours, or until thoroughly chilled. Then, in a separate bowl, put the egg whites, salt and cream of tartar. Beat the egg whites until stiff but not dry and fold into the chilled mixture. Pour mixture into your ice cream maker and proceed according to the directions of your own ice cream maker. Note the low calorie content and no preservatives. See why I recommend making your own ice milk!

sweets and desserts

CRUNCHY CAROB SAUCE

1/4 cup thinly sliced almonds
1-1/2 cups low-fat milk
2 tablespoons butter or corn oil margarine
1/2 cup carob powder (firmly packed)
1/2 cup date "sugar"
1-1/2 teaspoons dry instant coffee
1/8 teaspoon salt

2 tablespoons unprocessed wheat bran
1 teaspoon vanilla extract

Makes 2 cups
1 tablespoon contains approximately:
.2 gram of fiber
40 calories

Preheat the oven to 350°. Put the almonds on a cookie sheet in the preheated oven for approximately 10 minutes or until a golden brown. Watch carefully as they burn easily. Set aside.

Pour the milk into a saucepan and put on medium heat so that it will be at the boiling point when you need it. In another saucepan melt the butter or margarine and add the carob powder, mixing thoroughly. When thoroughly blended remove from the heat and add the hot milk all at once, rapidly stirring the mixture with a wire whisk. Add all of the other ingredients except the toasted almonds and put back on medium heat. Bring to a simmer and continue to stir occasionally with the whisk until the sauce is slightly thickened, about 20 minutes. Remove from the heat and cool to desired temperature. Add the toasted almonds and mix well.

I usually use Crunchy Carob Sauce to make Frozen Bonbons. However, it also makes good hot fudge sundaes.

HOT DATE BUTTER SUNDAE

1/4 cup chopped walnuts or almonds
1/2 cup Date Butter, page 49
2 cups Date "Sugar" Ice Milk, page 169

Makes 4 servings
Each serving contains approximately:
1.5 grams of fiber
304 calories

Preheat the oven to 350°. Put chopped walnuts or almonds on a cookie sheet in the preheated oven for approximately 10 minutes or until a golden brown. Watch carefully as they burn easily. Set aside. Put the Date Butter in a saucepan on low heat, stirring occasionally, for about 5 minutes. When warm through, remove from the heat and set aside.

Put 1/2 cup ice milk in each of 4 sherbet glasses. Spoon 2 tablespoons of the warm Date Butter and sprinkle 1 teaspoon of the toasted walnuts or almonds on the top of each sundae.

FUNNY BROWNIES

1 egg, beaten
1 cup date "sugar"
4 tablespoons butter or corn oil margarine,
   melted
1 teaspoon vanilla extract
1/4 cup chopped dates
3 tablespoons carob powder
1/4 cup rolled oats
1/4 cup whole wheat pastry flour

1/2 teaspoon baking powder
1/2 teaspoon salt
1/2 teaspoon ground cinnamon
1/4 cup unsweetened shredded coconut

Makes 36 brownies
Each brownie contains approximately:
.3 gram of fiber
46 calories

Preheat the oven to 325°. Combine the egg and date "sugar" and allow to stand for 10 minutes. Add melted butter, vanilla extract and chopped dates and mix well. In another bowl combine all other ingredients and mix well. Pour the dry ingredients into the wet ingredients (this saves 2 *really* messy bowls) and mix thoroughly. Pour the batter into a lightly buttered 8-inch square baking dish and press into shape with your fingers. Make sure the batter covers the entire surface of the pan evenly. Place the pan in the center of the preheated oven and bake for approximately 30 minutes, or until a toothpick inserted in the center comes out clean.

     Remove from the oven and place the baking dish on a cake rack to cool for 5 minutes before cutting brownies into squares. (Brownies should be sliced while still warm.) Cut into 36 squares and remove them with a spatula.

sweets and desserts

TOLL-FREE COOKIES

1/4 pound butter or corn oil margarine, at
   room temperature
3/4 cup date "sugar"
1 teaspoon vanilla extract
1 egg, beaten
1 cup whole wheat pastry flour
1/2 teaspoon salt
1/2 teaspoon baking soda

1 cup carob chips
1/2 cup chopped walnuts

Makes 4 dozen cookies
2 cookies contain approximately:
.4 gram of fiber
110 calories

Preheat the oven to 375°. Combine butter or margarine, date "sugar" and vanilla extract in a large mixing bowl. Using a pastry blender, mix until a creamy consistency. Add the beaten egg and mix well. Allow to stand for 10 minutes. Combine flour, salt and soda and add to the butter mixture, mixing well with a spoon. Stir in the carob chips and chopped nuts. Drop by half teaspoonfuls onto greased cookie sheets. Bake in the preheated oven for 8 to 10 minutes.

FIG BARS

3 eggs, beaten
1/2 cup date "sugar"
1 teaspoon vanilla extract
3/4 cup whole wheat flour
1/4 cup unprocessed wheat bran
1 teaspoon baking powder
1/8 teaspoon salt
1 teaspoon ground cinnamon

1/4 teaspoon ground nutmeg
1-1/2 cups finely chopped dried figs

Makes 36 fig bars
Each fig bar contains approximately:
.5 gram of fiber
40 calories

Preheat oven to 325°. Combine beaten eggs, date "sugar," and vanilla and allow to stand for 10 minutes. Combine flour, bran, baking powder, salt, cinnamon and nutmeg in a large mixing bowl and mix well. Pour the egg mixture into the dry ingredients. Add the chopped figs and mix thoroughly. Grease and flour a 9- by 13-inch baking dish, spoon the dough into the baking dish and spread evenly. Bake in the preheated oven for 25 minutes. Cool for about 10 minutes before cutting. Fig bars should be cut while they are still warm.

     These taste just like old-fashioned fig cookies and are great for school lunches, tea parties or just to fill the cookie jar.

SESAME SNAPS

3/4 cup hulled sesame seeds
1 egg, beaten
1-1/2 teaspoons vanilla extract
3/4 cup date "sugar"
3/4 cup butter or corn oil margarine,
  at room temperature
1 cup whole wheat flour

1/4 teaspoon salt
1/2 teaspoon baking powder

Makes 4 dozen cookies
2 cookies contain approximately:
.5 gram of fiber
138 calories

Preheat the oven to 350°. Place the sesame seeds on a cookie sheet in the preheated oven for 15 minutes or until a golden brown in color. Cool before using and set aside. Combine the beaten egg, vanilla extract and date "sugar" and allow to stand for 10 minutes. Cream butter or margarine and date "sugar" mixture in a large mixing bowl.

Combine the flour, salt and baking powder and add to creamed mixture a little at a time until it is all mixed in the dough. Add the toasted sesame seeds and again mix well. Drop by teaspoonfuls onto a greased cookie sheet, spacing cookies about 1 inch apart. Bake in a 350° oven for 15 minutes or until lightly browned.

CARTER CANDY

1/2 cup date "sugar"
1 cup unhomogenized peanut butter
1 egg white
1/2 teaspoon vanilla extract

Makes 36 candies
2 candies contain approximately:
.5 gram of fiber
54 calories

Cream date "sugar" and peanut butter together using a pastry blender. Put the egg white and vanilla in a separate bowl and beat very lightly with a fork, just enough to mix vanilla and egg white together. Add egg white to peanut butter mixture and mix well. All liquid should be absorbed. Form dough into a ball and wrap tightly. Refrigerate for 24 hours before baking.

Preheat oven to 300°. Separate the dough into 36 little balls and place them on an ungreased cookie sheet. Press each one down slightly with the tines of a fork. Bake for 10 minutes in the preheated oven. Allow to cool completely on the cookie sheet. Remove the candy with a metal spatula, being careful as they are quite fragile.

beverages

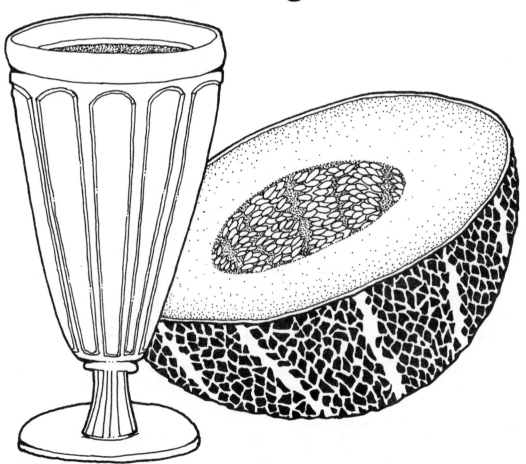

When thinking of foods high in dietary fiber we usually think of foods we can chew rather than drink. In this beverage section you will be surprised to find so many unusual, high fiber and delicious drinks. Surprise your friends with a Fabulous Fresh Fruit Smoothie, Dieter's Date Shake—or try my own favorite, Peanut Butter Punch!

PEANUT BUTTER PUNCH

1 cup low-fat milk
2 tablespoons unhomogenized peanut butter
1 tablespoon date "sugar"
1 teaspoon unprocessed wheat bran
1 teaspoon vanilla extract
4 ice cubes
ground cinnamon or nutmeg for garnish
   (optional)

Makes 2 servings
Each serving contains approximately:
.9 gram of fiber
121 calories

Put all ingredients in a blender and blend until smooth and creamy. Pour into 2 chilled glasses and sprinkle a little cinnamon or nutmeg on the top of each serving if desired.

    I have long been considered a real "peanut butter addict." I love peanut butter just plain or with fruit, sandwiches, pancakes, hamburgers, even omelets. Now for all of us who share this mania I have come up with a way we can drink it. Peanut Butter Punch is not only a delicious and unusual beverage, but it also has a high fiber content.

TOM'S EGG NOG

3 cups low-fat milk
2 eggs, dipped in boiling water for 30 seconds
1 tablespoon unprocessed wheat bran
1/2 teaspoon vanilla extract
1/2 teaspoon rum extract
1/2 teaspoon ground coriander
1/4 teaspoon ground nutmeg
1/4 teaspoon ground cinnamon

1 tablespoon date "sugar"
1/2 cup crushed ice
ground nutmeg for garnish

Makes 3 servings
Each serving contains approximately:
.4 gram of fiber
190 calories

Put all ingredients in a blender and blend until frothy. Serve in chilled glasses and sprinkle nutmeg over the top.

beverages

DESERT DATE SHAKE

3/4 cup chopped pitted dates
1-1/4 cups low-fat milk
2 cups Date "Sugar" Ice Milk

Makes 4 servings
Each serving contains approximately:
1.5 grams of fiber
267 calories

Put dates in a blender with 1/2 cup of the milk. Blend on high speed until mixture is almost smooth. Add the remaining milk and the ice milk and blend on low speed until just mixed. Serve immediately in chilled glasses.

DIETER'S DATE SHAKE

2/3 cup chopped pitted dates
1-1/2 cups non-fat milk
1 cup Jelled Milk, page 47
1 teaspoon vanilla extract
6 ice cubes
ground cinnamon or nutmeg for garnish
   (optional)

Makes 4 servings
Each serving contains approximately:
.9 gram of fiber
173 calories

Put dates in a blender with 1/2 cup of the milk. Blend on high speed until mixture is almost smooth. Add the remaining milk, Jelled Milk, vanilla extract and ice cubes. Blend until a thick creamy consistency.

   Pour into chilled glasses and sprinkle a little cinnamon or nutmeg on top of each shake if desired.

CANTALOUPE SMOOTHIE

1/2 cup unsweetened pineapple juice
1 cup diced cantaloupe
1 teaspoon unprocessed wheat bran
3 ice cubes

Makes 2 servings
Each serving contains approximately:
.3 gram of fiber
48 calories

Put all ingredients in a blender and blend until smooth. This is a very light and refreshing drink. I have been told that it is also delicious with a little rum added to it.

FABULOUS FRESH FRUIT SMOOTHIE

1 cup fresh orange juice
1 cup chopped pineapple
1 banana, sliced
1 cup low-fat milk
1 tablespoon date "sugar"
4 teaspoons unprocessed wheat bran
1 teaspoon vanilla extract

3 ice cubes
mint sprigs for garnish (optional)

Makes 4 servings
Each serving contains approximately:
.6 gram of fiber
105 calories

Put all ingredients in a blender and blend until smooth. Pour into 4 chilled glasses and garnish with a sprig of fresh mint, if desired. This is my own favorite smoothie.

BANANA BREAKFAST SHAKE

1 cup low-fat milk
1 banana
1 egg, dipped in boiling water for
   30 seconds
3 tablespoons defatted wheat germ
3 tablespoons unprocessed wheat bran
2 teaspoons date "sugar"

1 teaspoon vanilla extract

Makes 2 servings
Each serving contains approximately:
1.4 grams of fiber
207 calories

Put all ingredients in a blender and blend until smooth.

PINEAPPLE-"COCONUT" PUNCH

1 cup unsweetened pineapple juice
1/2 cup low-fat Jelled Milk, page 47
2 teaspoons unprocessed wheat bran
2 teaspoons date "sugar"
1/2 teaspoon vanilla extract
1/4 teaspoon coconut extract

ground cinnamon for garnish

Makes 2 servings
Each serving contains approximately:
.4 gram of fiber
110 calories

Put all ingredients in a blender and blend until smooth. Pour over ice in 2 tall glasses. Sprinkle a little cinnamon on the top of each drink.

beverages

CAROB COOLER

1 cup non-fat milk
1 tablespoon carob powder
1 teaspoon dry instant coffee
1 teaspoon unprocessed wheat bran
1/4 teaspoon ground cinnamon
1/2 teaspoon vanilla extract
4 teaspoons date "sugar"

4 ice cubes
cinnamon sticks for garnish (optional)

Makes 2 servings
Each serving contains approximately:
.7 gram of fiber
100 calories

Put all ingredients in a blender and blend until smooth and frothy. Serve in chilled glasses over ice and garnish with cinnamon sticks for a fancier presentation.

This is also a clever variation for a brunch drink to replace the more traditional fizz. Just add rum and offer your guests a "high fiber cocktail"!

fabulous facts

In each of my other books I have a recipe invention of my own which I can no longer do without. In *The Calculating Cook* it is Jelled Milk, which is the base of many sauces, whips and other low-calorie, rich-tasting concoctions. In *Diet for a Happy Heart* it is my Brown Sauce, a copy of the fabulous French original containing a fraction of the calories and no cholesterol. I have included both of these recipes (the Brown-Bran Sauce as a variation on the Brown Sauce) in this book because I have been unable to find a better method for cutting calories and still achieving the rich-tasting results than these two recipes already offer. I have also included a newly discovered method for making pie crusts which I am sure will join ranks with Jelled Milk and Brown Sauce and appear in my next book!

The stock recipes in this book remain the same as they appeared in my other books. I feel there is no reason to change recipes I worked so hard to perfect strictly for the sake of change—especially when basic stocks are so important to so many recipes. I have also included the same methods for toasting seeds, nuts, bread crumbs, croutons and tortillas. All of the other recipes are totally new and offer a whole new dimension to a healthier, happier life style.

Because fresh herbs are often unavailable, I have given measurements for dried unless fresh herbs are specified, with the exception of parsley and chives. I use a great deal of parsley for garnish, as well as an ingredient, and to have it readily on hand I always keep fresh parsley in a glass of water in the refrigerator and minced parsley in the freezer. If you have a choice between dried parsley and no parsley, no parsley is a far better flavor. Frozen parsley, when thawed, is almost as good as freshly cut parsley. Many other herbs can also be successfully stored in the freezer: mint, tarragon, cilantro, rosemary and basil to name a few. Just be sure they are kept in tightly sealed containers.

Because it is sometimes difficult to find fresh ginger root when you want it, always try to keep it in your freezer. Peel the whole ginger root and grate it, using what you need and putting the remaining ginger in a sealed plastic bag for future use.

Vegetables and fruits are always used unpeeled unless otherwise specified, with the exception of onions, garlic and bananas. All nuts should be raw and unpeeled unless otherwise indicated.

In recipes calling for butter I always give corn oil margarine as an alternative. In specifying the *corn oil* margarine I mean pure corn oil margarine without preservatives or additives. It is not 179

fabulous facts

as readily available as corn oil margarine with additives, and needs to be searched for in your market.

I always store flour and grains in tightly covered containers in the refrigerator to preserve their freshness and avoid worry of weevils or other little creatures who also enjoy their flavor.

Date "sugar" may be used as you would any other sugar, sprinkled on cereal, fruits or used in cooking. However, when you are baking, date "sugar" should always be added to the liquid ingredients and allowed to stand for 10 minutes before combining it with the other ingredients. This will reconstitute the date "sugar" so it will not burn before the other ingredients are thoroughly cooked. When using date "sugar" in recipes where the ingredients are toasted, such as granola, add it halfway through the cooking time so it will not burn before the other ingredients are adequately toasted.

KITCHEN VOCABULARY

FOR PREPARATION

CHOP Using a large chopping knife, hold point end down with one hand and use the other hand to chop. There are also chopping devices available in most appliance and hardware stores.
COARSELY CHOP Chop in pieces approximately 1/2-inch square.
FINELY CHOP Chop in pieces approximately 1/4-inch square.
MINCE Chop as fine as gravel.
CUBE Cut into cube-shaped pieces approximately 1 inch or specified size.
DICE Cut into 1/4-inch cubes or smaller.
SLICE Using a sharp knife, slice through evenly to specified thickness.
THINLY SLICE Using the slicing side for very thinly sliced vegetables of a 4-sided grater, slice vegetables such as cucumbers and onions.

JULIENNE CUT Cut in strips approximately 1/4 inch by 2 inches.

SNIP Cut into small pieces using scissors or kitchen shears.

SCORE Using a knife, make shallow cuts or slits on surface.

SHRED Slice thinly in 2 directions, or use a shredder.

GRATE Rub the surface to be grated on grater for desired-size particles. For example, finely grated and coarsely grated would require 2 different size graters.

GRIND Use a food chopper or grinder.

CRUMBLE Crush with your hands or a fork into crumblings, food such as toast, farmer cheese, et cetera.

PRESS This term applies usually to garlic when using a garlic press.

CRUSH Using a mortar and pestle, crush dry herbs before using.

MASH Potatoes and many other cooked vegetables can be mashed using a potato masher, or brought to the same consistency in an electric blender or mixer.

PEEL Remove outer covering of food such as oranges, lemons and bananas.

PARE Using a knife, remove the outer covering of food such as apples and peaches.

SCRAPE Scrape to remove outer skin on food such as carrots and parsnips, or scrape to produce juice in food such as onions.

SKIN Remove skin of such food as chicken; sometimes used when referring to onions.

CORE Remove core from fruits such as pears and apples.

PIT Remove the pit or seed from fruits such as peaches and plums.

SEED Completely remove small seeds from such foods as tomatoes, cucumbers and bell peppers.

FILLET Remove *all* bones; usually refers to fish.

BONE Remove *all* bones; usually refers to roasts and poultry.

STIR Using a spoon in a circular motion until all ingredients are well mixed.

TOSS Mix from both sides in an under and over motion toward the center, using 2 spoons or a fork and spoon; usually refers to salads.

FOLD IN Using a rubber spatula or spoon in a circular motion coming across the bottom, fold the bottom over the top. Repeat slowly until mixture is folded in as indicated in the recipe.

KNEAD Usually referring to bread dough. After mixing dough according to recipe, place on a floured surface, flatten ball of dough with floured hands and fold it toward you. With the heels of your hands, press down and flatten again. Continue doing this until dough is smooth and satiny, or as recipe directs.

CREAM With a spoon, rub against sides of bowl until creamy. A pastry blender may also be used.

DISSOLVE Mix dry ingredients with liquid until no longer visible in the solution.

WHISK Stir, beat or fold using a wire whisk.

WHIP Beat rapidly with fork, whisk, egg beater or electric mixer to add air and increase volume of mixture.

BEAT Using egg beater or electric mixer, beat to add air and increase volume.

STIFFLY BEATEN Beat until mixture stands in stiff peaks.

STIFF BUT NOT DRY This term is often used for egg whites and means they should hold soft, well-defined peaks but not be beaten to the point where they look as though they will break.

BLEND Combine 2 or more ingredients well; often used when referring to an electric blender.

BLEND UNTIL FROTHY This is a term I use meaning to blend until the volume is almost doubled by the addition of air and is foamy.

PURÉE Put through a fine sieve or food mill, or use an electric blender.

SPRINKLE Just as the word implies, sprinkle, using your fingers as directed in recipe.

DOT Scatter in small bits over surface of food, actually "sprinkling," and usually refers to butter or margarine.

DREDGE Sprinkle lightly with flour, or coat with flour.

COAT Using a sifter, sprinkle ingredient with flour, sugar substitute, et cetera, until coated. Roll in flour or shake in a paper bag until coated.

181

fabulous facts

SIFT Put flour, sugar, et cetera, through a flour sifter or sieve.

GREASE Rub lightly with margarine, corn oil, et cetera.

COOL Allow to stand at room temperature until no longer warm to the touch.

CHILL Place in refrigerator until cold.

MARINATE Allow mixture to stand in marinade for length of time indicated in recipe.

SKEWER Hold together with metal or wooden skewers, or spear chunks of meat/vegetables on wooden skewers, such as for shish kabob.

FOR COOKING

PREHEAT Set oven to desired temperature. Wait until temperature is reached before baking.

BAKE Cook in heated oven.

ROAST To bake meat or poultry.

BROIL Cook under broiler at designated distance.

BARBECUE Cook over hot coals.

TOAST Brown in a toaster, oven or under broiler. When applied to nuts, seeds or coconut, these may be toasted in a 350° oven until desired color is attained. Or, place under broiler and if this method is used watch carefully as they will burn quickly.

BROWN Brown in oven under a broiler or in a heavy iron skillet to desired color.

SEAR Brown surface rapidly over high heat in a hot skillet.

SINGE Usually refers to poultry. Hold over flame to burn off all hairs.

FRY Cook in a small amount of oil in a skillet.

PAN BROIL Cook in ungreased or cured hot skillet pouring off fat as it accumulates.

DEEP FRY Use a deep-fat fryer, adding enough oil to cover food to be cooked. If temperature is given in the recipe, a deep-fat frying thermometer will be needed.

SAUTÉ Cook in small amount of hot oil in a skillet.

BRAISE Brown meat well on all sides, adding a small amount of water or other liquid. Cover and simmer over low heat or place in a moderate oven and cook until tender or as recipe directs.

BOIL Cook food in liquid in which bubbles constantly rise to the surface and break. At sea level, water boils at 212° F.

SIMMER Cook just below boiling point at about 185° F at sea level.

SCALD Heat to just under the boiling point where tiny bubbles start at the side. This is also often called "bring to boiling point."

STEAM To cook food over boiling water using either a steamer or a large kettle with a rack placed in the bottom of it to hold the pan or dish of food above the boiling water.

STEEP Allow to stand in hot liquid.

CODDLE Usually used when referring to eggs. When a raw egg is called for in a recipe such as eggnog, Caesar salad, et cetera, put the egg in boiling water for 30 seconds before using it. The reason for coddling the egg is that avedin, a component of raw egg whites, is believed to block the absorption of biotin, one of the water soluble vitamins. Avedin is extremely sensitive to heat and coddling the egg inactivates the avedin.

PARBOIL Boil in water or other liquid until partially cooked. This is usually done before another form of cooking.

POACH Cook for a short time in simmering liquid.

BLANCH To dip quickly into boiling water. Usually refers to fruits and vegetables. When referring to nuts, cover shelled nuts with cold water and bring to a boil. Remove from heat and drain. Slip skins from nuts.

BASTE Spoon liquid over food while it is cooking as directed, or use a baster.

THICKEN Mix thickening agent, arrowroot, cornstarch, flour, et cetera, with a small amount of the liquid to be thickened and add slowly to the hot liquid, stirring constantly. Cook until slightly thickened or until mixture coats a metal spoon.

FORK TENDER When food can be easily pierced with a fork.

COVER TIGHTLY Sealed so that steam cannot escape.

equivalents

BEVERAGES
Ice cubes
2 ice cubes = 1/4 cup
8 ice cubes = 1 cup
Instant coffee
4-ounce jar = 60 cups coffee
Coffee
1 pound (80 tablespoons) = 40 to
50 cups
Tea leaves
1 pound = 300 cups tea

FATS
Miscellaneous
Bacon, 1 pound, rendered = 1-1/2 cups
Bacon, 1 slice, cooked crisp =
1 tablespoon, crumbled
Butter, 1 cube (1/4 pound) = 1/2 cup
or 8 tablespoons
Cheese, cream, 3-ounce package =
6 tablespoons
Cream, heavy whipping, 1 cup =
2 cups, whipped
Margarine, 1 cube (1/4 pound) =
1/2 cup or 8 tablespoons
Nuts in the shell
Almonds, 1 pound = 1 cup nutmeats
Brazil nuts, 1 pound = 1-1/2 cups
nutmeats
Peanuts, 1 pound = 2 cups nutmeats
Pecans, 1 pound = 2-1/2 cups nutmeats
Walnuts, 1 pound = 2-1/2 cups
nutmeats
Nuts, shelled
Almonds, 1/2 pound = 2 cups

Almonds, 42, chopped = 1/2 cup
Brazil nuts, 1/2 pound = 1-1/2 cups
Coconut, 1/2 pound, shredded =
2-1/2 cups
Macadamia nuts, 3,
finely chopped = 1 tablespoon
Peanuts, 1/2 pound = 1 cup
Pecans, 1/2 pound = 2 cups
Walnuts, 1/2 pound = 2 cups
Walnuts, 15, chopped = 1/2 cup

FRUITS (DRIED)
Apricots, 24 halves, 1 cup = 1-1/2
cups, cooked
Dates, 1 pound, 2-1/2 cups = 1-3/4
cups, pitted and chopped
Figs, 1 pound, 2-1/2 cups = 4-1/2
cups, cooked
Pears, 1 pound, 3 cups = 5-1/2 cups,
cooked
Prunes, pitted, 1 pound, 2-1/2 cups =
3-3/4 cups, cooked
Raisins, seedless, 1 pound, 2-3/4
cups = 3-3/4 cups, cooked

FRUITS (FRESH)
Apples, 1 pound, 4 small =
3 cups, chopped
Apricots, 1 pound, 6 to 8
average = 2 cups, chopped
Bananas, 1 pound, 4 small =
2 cups, mashed
Berries, 1 pint = 2 cups

Cantaloupe, 2 pounds, 1 average =
3 cups, diced
Cherries, 1 pint = 1 cup, pitted
Cranberries, 1 pound = 4-1/2 cups
Crenshaw melon, 3 pounds, 1 average =
4-1/2 cups, diced
Figs, 1 pound, 4 small = 2 cups,
chopped
Grapefruit, 1 small = 1 cup,
sectioned
Grapes, Concord, 1/4 pound,
30 grapes = 1 cup
Grapes, Thompson seedless,
1/4 pound, 40 grapes = 1 cup
Guavas, 1 pound, 4 medium = 1 cup
chopped
Honeydew melon, 2 pounds, 1 average
= 3 cups, diced
Kumquats, 1 pound, 8 to 10 average =
2 cups, sliced
Lemon, 1 medium (3 average =
1 pound) = 3 tablespoons juice;
2 teaspoons grated peel
Limes, 1/2 pound, 5 average =
4 tablespoons juice; 4 to 5 teaspoons grated peel
Loquats, 1 pound, 5 average =
1-1/2 cups, chopped
Lychees, 1 pound, 6 average =
1/2 cup, chopped
Mangoes, 1 pound, 2 average =
1-1/2 cups, chopped
Nectarines, 1 pound, 3 average =
2 cups, chopped

equivalents

Orange, 1 small (2 average = 1 pound)
= 6 tablespoons juice; 1 tablespoon
grated peel, 3/4 cup sectioned
Papaya, 1 medium = 1-1/2 cups,
chopped
Peaches, 1 pound, 3 average =
2 cups, chopped
Pears, 1 pound, 3 average = 2 cups,
chopped
Persimmons, 1 pound, 3 average =
2 cups, mashed
Pineapple, 3 pounds, 1 medium =
2-1/2 cups, chopped
Plums, 1 pound, 4 average = 2 cups,
chopped
Pomegranate, 1/4 pound, 1 average =
3 cups seeds
Prunes, 1 pound, 5 average =
2 cups, chopped
Rhubarb, 1 pound, 4 slender stalks =
2 cups, cooked
Tangerines, 1 pound, 4 average =
2 cups, sectioned
Watermelon, 10 to 12 pounds,
1 average = 20 to 24 cups, cubed

HERBS, SPICES AND SEASONINGS
Garlic powder, 1/8 teaspoon =
1 small clove garlic
Ginger, powdered, 1/2 teaspoon =
1 teaspoon, fresh
Herbs, dried, 1/2 teaspoon =
1 tablespoon, fresh
Horseradish, bottled, 2 tablespoons = 1 tablespoon, fresh

MILK
Dry, whole powdered milk, 1/4 cup
+ 1 cup water = 1 cup whole milk

Dry, non-fat powdered milk, 1/3 cup
+ 2/3 cup water = 1 cup non-fat
milk
Skimmed, canned, 1 cup =
5 cups, whipped

PROTEIN
Cheese
Cottage cheese, 1/2 pound = 1 cup
Cheese, grated, 1/4 pound = 1 cup
Eggs and Egg Substitutes
Eggs, raw, whole, 6 medium = 1 cup
Eggs, raw, in shell, 10 medium =
1 pound
Egg whites, 1 medium = 1-1/2
tablespoons
Egg whites, 9 medium = 1 cup
Egg yolks, 1 medium = 1 tablespoon
Egg yolks, 16 medium = 1 cup
Egg, hard-cooked, 1 =
1/3 cup, finely chopped
Egg substitute, liquid, 1/4 cup =
1 egg (see label)
Egg substitute, dry, 3 tablespoons =
1 egg (see label)
Seafood and Fish
Crab, fresh or frozen, cooked or
canned, 1/2 pound (5-1/2- to
7-1/2-ounce tin) = 1 cup
Escargots, 6 snails = 1-1/2 ounces
Lobster, fresh or frozen, cooked,
1/2 pound = 1 cup
Oysters, raw, 1/2 pound = 1 cup
Scallops, fresh or frozen, shucked,
1/2 pound = 1 cup
Shrimp, cooked, 1 pound = 3 cups
Tuna, drained, canned, 6-1/2 to
7 ounces = 3/4 cup

STARCHES
Crumbs
Bread crumbs, soft, 1 slice = 3/4 cup
Bread crumbs, dry, crumbled, 2 slices =
1/2 cup
Bread crumbs, dry, ground, 4 slices =
1/2 cup
Graham crackers, 14 squares, fine
crumbs = 1 cup
Soda crackers, 21 squares, fine
crumbs = 1 cup
Cereals and Noodles
Flour, cake, 1 pound = 4-1/2 cups,
sifted
Flour, all-purpose, 1 pound =
4 cups, sifted
Bulgur, 1/3 cup = 1 cup, cooked
Cornmeal, 1 cup = 4 cups, cooked
Macaroni, 1 pound, 5 cups =
12 cups, cooked
Noodles, 1 pound, 5-1/2 cups =
10 cups, cooked
Oatmeal, quick-cooking, 1 cup =
2 cups, cooked
Spaghetti, 1 pound = 9 cups, cooked

STOCK BASE AND
BOUILLON CUBES
Beef Stock Base, Powdered
1 teaspoon = 1 bouillon cube
4 teaspoons + 1-1/4 cups water =
1 10-1/2-ounce can bouillon,
undiluted
1 teaspoon + 5 ounces water =
5 ounces stock
1 teaspoon + 1 cup water =
1 cup bouillon
Chicken Stock Base, Powdered
1 teaspoon = 1 bouillon cube

equivalents

1 teaspoon + 5 ounces water =
5 ounces stock
1 teaspoon + 1 cup water =
1 cup bouillon

VEGETABLES (DRIED)
Garbanzo beans, 1 pound, 2 cups =
6 cups, cooked
Kidney beans, 1 pound, 1-1/2 cups =
9 cups, cooked
Lima or navy beans, 1 pound,
2-1/2 cups = 6 cups, cooked
Rice, 1 pound, 2-1/2 cups =
8 cups, cooked
Split peas, 1 pound, 2 cups =
5 cups, cooked

VEGETABLES (FRESH)
Artichokes, 1/2 pound = 1 average
Asparagus, 1 pound, 18 spears =
2 cups, cut in 1-inch pieces
Avocado, 1 medium = 2 cups, chopped
Beans, green, 1 pound = 3 cups,
chopped and cooked
Beets, 1 pound, medium-size =
2 cups, cooked and sliced
Bell pepper, 1/2 pound, 1 large =
1 cup, seeded and finely chopped
Broccoli, 1 pound, 2 stalks = 6 cups,
chopped and cooked
Brussels sprouts, 1 pound, 28 average =
4 cups
Cabbage, 1 pound = 4 cups, shredded;
2-1/2 cups, cooked
Carrots, 1 pound, 8 small = 4 cups,
chopped
Cauliflower, 1-1/2 pounds, 1 average =
6 cups, chopped and cooked

Celery, 1 stalk = 1/2 cup, finely chopped
Celery root, 1-3/4 pounds, 1 average =
4 cups raw, grated; 2 cups,
cooked and mashed
Corn, 6 ears = 1-1/2 cups, cut
Cucumber, 1 medium = 1-1/2 cups, sliced
Eggplant, 1 pound, 1 medium =
12 1/4-inch slices; 6 cups, cubed
Lettuce, 1 average head = 6 cups,
bite-size pieces
Lima beans, baby, 1 pound = 2 cups
Mushrooms, fresh, 1/2 pound,
20 medium = 2 cups raw, sliced
Okra, 24 medium = 1/2 pound
Onion, 1 medium = 1 cup, finely
chopped
Parsnips, 1 pound, 6 average =
4 cups, chopped
Peas, in pods, 1 pound = 1 cup,
shelled and cooked
Pimiento, 1 4-ounce jar = 1/2 cup,
chopped
Potatoes, 1 pound, 4 medium =
2-1/2 cups, cooked and diced
Pumpkin, 3 pounds, 1 average piece =
4 cups, cooked and mashed
Rutabagas, 1-1/2 pounds, 3 small =
2 cups, cooked and mashed
Spinach, 1 pound = 3-1/2 cups,
uncooked; 1 cup, cooked
Squash, acorn, 1-1/2 pounds, 1 average
= 2 cups, cooked and mashed
Squash, banana, 3 pounds, 1 average
piece = 4 cups, cooked and mashed
Squash, summer, 1 pound, 4 average =
1 cup, cooked
Squash, zucchini, 1 pound, 2 average =
1-1/4 cups, cooked and chopped;
3 cups raw, diced

Tomatoes, 1 pound, 3 medium =
1-1/4 cups, cooked and chopped
Turnips, white, 1 pound, 3 small =
2 cups, peeled and grated;
1-1/4 cups, cooked and mashed

MISCELLANEOUS
Chocolate, 1 square, 1 ounce =
4 tablespoons, grated
Gelatin, sheet, 4 sheets = 1 envelope
Gelatin, powdered, 1/4-ounce envelope
= 1 scant tablespoon
Yeast, fresh, 1 package = 2 tablespoons
Yeast, dry, 1 envelope (to be recon-
stituted in 2 tablespoons water) =
1-3/4 tablespoons

METRIC WEIGHTS
For Dry Measure
Convert known ounces into grams by
multiplying by 28
Convert known pounds into kilograms
by multiplying by .45
Convert known grams into ounces by
multiplying by .035
Convert known kilograms into pounds
by multiplying by 2.2
For Liquid Measure
Convert known ounces into milli-
liters by multiplying by 30
Convert known pints into liters by
multiplying by .47
Convert known quarts into liters by
multiplying by .95
Convert known gallons into liters
by multiplying by 3.8
Convert known milliliters into ounces
by multiplying by .034

185

bibliography

Bowes & Church. *Food Values of Portions Commonly Used,* 11th ed. Philadelphia: J. B. Lippincott Company, 1970.

Flath, F.A.C.H.A., F.A.P.H.A., Carl I. *The Miracle Nutrient.* New York: M. Evans & Co., 1975.

Fredericks, Carlton. *High-Fiber Way to Total Health.* New York: Pocket Books, 1976.

Heaton, K.W. "Are We Getting Too Much Out of Food?" *Nutrition.* 27 (1973): 170.

Jones, Jeanne. *The Calculating Cook.* San Francisco: 101 Productions, 1972.

Jones, Jeanne. *Diet for a Happy Heart.* San Francisco: 101 Productions, 1975.

Kraus, Barbara. *Guide to Fiber in Foods.* New York: New American Library, 1975.

Reuben, M.D., David. *The Save-Your-Life Diet.* New York: Random House, 1975.

Siegal, D.O., M.D., Sanford. *Dr. Siegal's Natural Fiber Cookbook.* New York: The Dial Press/James Wade, 1976.

Siegal, D.O., M.D., Sanford. *Dr. Siegal's Natural Fiber Permanent Weight-Loss Diet.* New York: Dell Publishing Co., Inc., 1975.

Stanway, M.B., M.R.C.P., Andrew. *Taking the Rough with the Smooth.* London: Souvenir Press Ltd., 1976.

"Composition of Foods—Raw, Processed, Prepared," *Revised U.S.D.A. Agricultural Handbook,* Number 8, 1973.

Wade, Carlson. *The Book of Bran.* New York: Pyramid Books, 1976.

Wason, Betty. *High-Fiber Cookbook.* New York: Rawson Associates, 1976.

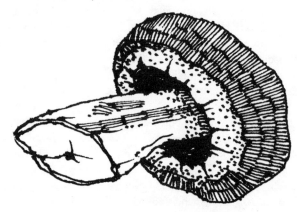

index

index

index

biographical notes

JEANNE JONES has achieved an international reputation for combining creative cooking with sound nutritional practices in her recipes and diet programs. Her first book *The Calculating Cook* was published in 1972, followed by *Diet for a Happy Heart* in 1975.

Her serious interest in nutrition started when she was placed on a diabetic diet herself and realized that this diet was not as restrictive as it first appeared but rather just a perfectly balanced diet. Refusing to relinquish her role as a gourmet cook and hostess she used her international background in foods and entertaining to create a unique approach to recipes and menus for others on restricted diets. The recipes became the basis for her book *The Calculating Cook: A Gourmet Cookbook for Diabetics and Dieters.* The book subsequently was approved for use by diabetics by the American Diabetes Association and was named the best adult book of the year by the National Federation of Press Women.

Realizing the interrelationship and interdependence between diabetes, fats and obesity and encouraged by many doctors she began work on *Diet for a Happy Heart,* a collection of recipes low in cholesterol, low in saturated fat and sugar free.

The growing awareness of the importance of dietary fiber to good health motivated Jeanne to expand her gourmet approach to better nutrition into the fiber-diet field. She has created delicious and unusual recipes high in dietary fiber, low in calories, sugar free and completely natural. As in her previous books she has worked closely with doctors and dieticians in developing this book.

Jeanne Jones also serves as a consultant on recipe development and menu planning for a number of health organizations, diet-food manufacturers and restaurants. She is a member of the editorial board of *Diabetes Forecast,* the official magazine of the American Diabetes Association; a member of the Board of Directors of the San Diego County Heart Association; and a member of the External Advisory Committee to the Diet Modification Program of the National Heart and Blood Vessel Research Demonstration Center in Houston.

Jeanne is a frequent lecturer throughout the world in the field of better diet and imaginative menu planning.

CATHY GREENE studied at Chouniard Art Institute in Los Angeles and presently works as a free-lance artist in Northern California. She has illustrated a number of other books, including *Small World Vegetable Gardening* (101 Productions) and garden books published by Simon and Schuster and Rodale Press.